The Six Thinking Hats® for schools and families

Inspiring Children and Young People to think for themselves

A guide for teachers, parents and guardians

Originator: Dr Edward de Bono
Updated by: Karen Draper and Caspar de Bono

Illustrations: Chan Yin
Covers and layout design: Elisa Garis

ISBN: 978-1-7397893-2-9

Published by Edward de Bono Ltd t/a de Bono. Registered office: First Floor, Templeback, 10 Temple Back, Bristol, BS1 6FL. Registered in England. Registered number: 11433091. Copyright 2023.

This material may only be copied according to the guidelines on page 2.

www.debono.com

Editor's Note

My father dedicated his life to teaching thinking as a skill. I learned how to think across the breakfast, lunch, and dinner table. When I find myself starting to say, 'There are two possibilities', I stop before I say 'two' and say 'three' instead, even though I don't know what the third possibility is yet. Try it - good thinking is about being willing to explore and develop new possibilities, not just describe what you already know.

Dr Edward de Bono started writing about thinking as a skill in 1967, publishing one or two books a year until 2018. He died in 2021 at the age of 88. A few months earlier, he took part in a virtual conference encouraging more self-directed thinking in education.

Many teachers and parents have asked me for updated versions of his thinking lessons for children. The first set of Thinking Lessons focuses on 'points of view' and is available for free in digital form at https://www.debono.com/de-bono-thinking-lessons-1. It comprises seven lessons on how to direct our attention so that we have a broader view of a situation before concluding.

The *Six Thinking Hats for schools and families* is the next title in the series. I am very grateful to Karen Draper for applying her considerable experience as a teacher to updating these materials. Also, my thanks to the team at Perfection Learning, who produced the first edition of *Six Thinking Hats for schools*.

I hope you enjoy making thinking an accessible, practical and valuable skill.

Caspar de Bono

Copying and Accreditation

Teachers, parents and guardians are welcome to copy of a few pages of this book for use with the children they are responsible for. Alternatively please purchase the student version. The material cannot be copied or reproduced in any manner for the benefit of a wider audience without the written permission of the copyright owner, Edward de Bono Ltd.

The **Six Thinking Hats** and **de Bono** are registered trademarks. If you wish to promote yourself or your school using the Six Thinking Hats for schools badge then you must become accredited in the method.

Please visit https://www.debono.com/6th-for-schools-and-families for more information about accreditation.

About the Originator and Contributor

Originator: Dr Edward de Bono

Dr Edward de Bono was a pioneer in the teaching of thinking. Having taught thinking skills to executives, children and Nobel Prize laureates alike, his influence was far-reaching. He wrote more than 60 books and teaching programmes (translated into 43 languages) lectured in 58 countries, and made three television series. His ideas have been adopted by major corporations and governments. The widespread and enduring use of Dr de Bono's methods across different cultures and contexts is due to the simplicity and usefulness of his ideas.

Dr de Bono held faculty appointments at Oxford, Cambridge, London and Harvard. He became interested in the nature and teaching of thinking while working in medical research. His investigations led to his description of the behaviour of the mind as a self-organising system and his interest in the development of lateral thinking to change perception. He described parallel thinking, also known as the Six Thinking Hats method as an alternative to argumentative thinking and a complement to 'what is' or descriptive thinking. Dr de Bono also emphasised the importance of thinking about 'what can be,' involving thinking constructively and creatively and purposefully 'designing a way forward'.

Contributor: Karen Draper

Karen has worked successfully across education sectors in England and Wales as a teacher, leader, adviser, inspector, and coach, always remaining passionate about education and its potential to impact every child and their community.

After gaining her BEd from Birmingham University at the age of 34, she became a primary school teacher. There she thrived, learned, and became as curious as she had been as a five-year-old. Karen soon became aware of the work of Dr Edward de Bono, specifically the Six Thinking Hats method. Her application of the system with both children and adults demonstrated that simple methods are powerful.

The Six Thinking Hats continues to inspire her in classrooms and staffrooms as well as in her personal life. She continues to pursue pedagogies that motivate and empower teachers, always trying to bring relevance to children's lived experience.

Karen believes that there is always opportunity to grow, adapt and think better; that parenting and teaching are two of the most influential and precious vocations; and that if we can harness the potential of our children, there is hope. Today's world needs confident and flexible thinkers who can adapt and add value to their societies.

Contents

Editor's Note 2
Copying and Accreditation 2
About the Originator and Contributor 3

1. The Purpose of the Hats

1.1 How to Use This Book 6
1.2 Six Hats Summary Sheet 7
1.3 Examples of Using the Six Thinking Hats in Practice 8
1.4 The Purpose and Benefits of Using the Six Thinking Hats 10
1.5 The Teaching of Thinking Skills 12
1.6 The Role of the Teacher 15
1.7 A Model Lesson Plan 19

2. Learning the Hats

The White Hat 24

The Red Hat 29

The Black Hat 34

Yellow Hat 39

The Green Hat 44

The Blue Hat 49

3. How to Use the Hats

3.1 The Systematic Use of the Thinking Hats 58
3.2 Six Thinking Hats Sequences 68
3.3 Experiencing Sequential Thinking 70

4. Additional Practice Topics

4.1 All-weather Bike 76
4.2 White Hat Practice 78
4.3 Red Hat Practice 80
4.4 Black Hat Practice 82
4.5 Yellow Hat Practice 84
4.6 Green Hat Practice 86
4.7 Blue Hat Practice 88
4.8 Additional Practice 92
4.9 Additional Practice for Families 94

1 The Purpose of the Hats

What do you think of the idea that all seats should be removed from buses?

Consider this question for a moment before reading on.

It is likely that you quickly concluded that this was a bad idea and reinforced this judgement with a few reasons. For example, people are more likely to hurt themselves if they are standing up. Removing the seats might be inconsiderate to people who need to sit down. It could be dangerous if standing up encouraged people to move around the bus while it is in motion. It might be harder for the driver to see out of the back. It would be tiring to stand throughout a long journey.

There is a simple thinking tool called PMI,[1] or plus, minus and interesting, whereby an individual or group of people spends two minutes focusing on the plus points of the idea, two minutes exploring only the issues and, finally, two minutes reflecting on the interesting points. What is fascinating, is that people often change their own minds about a topic when they use this tool. Although we think that we are objective and open-minded when we explore a topic, in practice, we often rush to judgement and use our intelligence to justify our point of view. A key principle of this method is that participants are not taking sides, for or against the idea, but are exploring the different implications in parallel. The Six Thinking Hats approach follows the same principles as the PMI method but does so across six modes of thinking.

Some of the plus points for taking the seats out of buses are that you can fit more people on the bus, it is quicker to board and exit, it is cheaper and easier to maintain and clean, and there is more space for bags and equipment.

Some of the interesting points are as follows: what do you do with the seats that have been taken out? Does the driver sit down or stand? Can you have seats that could be easily removed or added as needed? Is it possible to design a safe way for many people to stand on a bus?

The outcome of this approach is an opening of possibilities that can be further developed.

---

1. See the PMI lesson at https://www.debono.com/de-bono-thinking-lessons-1

1.1
How to Use This Book

'An idea that is developed and put into action is more important than an idea that exists only as an idea.'

Dr Edward de Bono

▬ A Practical Skill

You do not need to read this book cover to cover.

Thinking is a practical skill that requires both an understanding of the principles and the experience of practice. When teaching thinking skills, it is vital to use a variety of practice exercises so that the learner becomes familiar with the thinking skill rather than caught up in the detail of a single practice topic. There are many practice topics to choose from.

Pages 7-9 provide a broad understanding of how the hats work and it is recommended that everyone starts with this.

Pages 10-15 provide the purpose and principles of the method. Some people will want to know the deeper foundations before moving on, while others are welcome to return to this section later.

Section 2 provides a lesson plan on each hat. They do not have to be taught in this order, but we recommend that the blue hat be introduced last. Each lesson follows the model lesson plan explained on page 18. You are encouraged to adapt the practice exercises as appropriate to your context.

Section 3 discusses how to combine the hats into sequences or recipes for different situations. This is best approached once your learners are familiar with each of the hats. Pages 68-69 provide a brief overview of what is possible.

Section 4 contains additional practice topics to select from. There are alternatives to those presented in the lesson plans or opportunities for further practice.

1.2
Six Hats Summary Sheet

Red hat: Feelings.
What are my feelings about this?
(no justification needed)

Yellow hat: Strengths.
What are the good points?

Black hat: Weaknesses.
What do we need to be cautious about?

Green hat: New ideas.
What is possible?

White hat: Information.
What are the facts?

Blue hat: Thinking about thinking.
How might we organise the thinking?

Remember:
- Each hat stands for one mode of thinking.
- **It is essential that everyone use the same hat at the same time.**
- Use only the type of thinking indicated by that hat colour.
- You can put on or take off a hat. When you put on a hat, you play the role attached to that hat.
- You can ask someone else to put on a hat, take off a hat or switch hats.

1.3
Examples of Using the Six Thinking Hats in Practice

'It is better to have enough ideas for some of them to be wrong, than to be always right by having no ideas at all.'

Dr Edward de Bono

We recommend that you teach each of the hats individually first before putting them together, following the lessons provided in Section 2. The following examples illustrate how the hats can be combined to structure one's thinking.

▬ Six Hats for Broader Thinking

The Six Thinking Hats method allows learners to think more comprehensively. When we simply ask learners to think about something, they are often at a loss. But if they are invited to explore the subject using the framework of the hats, their perceptual powers quickly expand.

> Ask learners to read the poem and state their thoughts about it.

> *The icy air stings,*
> *warning an innocent world.*
> *Watch – winter wants you!*
>   Anonymous

Example Six Hats response

Red hat (feelings)

— 'I really like that poem.'
— 'It gives me a feeling of danger.'
— 'I can feel the sting of the air.'

White hat (facts)

— ''The poem has no title.'
— 'We don't know who wrote it.'
— 'It doesn't rhyme.'
— 'It has three lines.'
— ''The middle line is longest.'
— 'It's about winter coming.'
— ''The world is called 'innocent.'

Yellow hat (good points)

— 'The poet makes winter sound frightening. Winter sounds like an enemy, sneaking up.'
— 'The last line has a lot of "w" sounds: "watch", "winter", "wants". They make a whispering sound like the wind.'

1. The Purpose of the Hats

In another exercise, learners can be asked to respond to the following proposal:

> School should start one hour earlier in the morning and end one hour earlier.

Teacher: Let's have some red hat thinking. What are your feelings about that suggestion? Don't explain your reasons; just tell me what you feel.

Sample responses:
— I don't like it.
— I think it's a dumb idea.
— I think it's great.

(If learners find it difficult to respond, you can take a poll of their feelings. Raise your hand if you feel it is a good idea. Raise your hand if you feel it is a bad idea. Raise your hand if you feel it is an interesting idea.)

Teacher: Now, try the yellow hat. What are any benefits or good points of the idea?

Sample responses:
— Ending earlier might be good because you would have more of the day left.
— Getting to school might be easier because there would be less traffic at that time.

Teacher: Now for some black hat thinking. That means checking what is wrong with the idea and why the idea may not work. Let's have some suggestions.

Sample responses:
— People might not want to get up so early in the morning.
— Learners might be more tired during school.
— Starting school earlier might require children to walk or travel in the dark, which could be dangerous.

Teacher: What about some new ideas on this with some green hat thinking?

Sample responses:
— Perhaps learners, teachers and parents could all vote on what time they wanted their school to start.
— Maybe the earlier starting time could be tried out for one week to see how it works.

Teacher: Now for the white hat thinking. What information should we have to think about this suggestion?

Sample responses:
— We should find out how early the buses start running.
— We should find out when it gets light at different times of the year.

Teacher: Finally, the blue hat. What thinking plan have we used to talk about the early school proposal? Which hat did we wear first? Second? What was the sequence?

Sample responses:
— First, we used the red, to see how we felt about the proposal. Then yellow, to look at the good points. Then black, to find what was wrong with the idea. Then, we used the green hat, to think of new ideas, and then the white and blue hats.

1.4 The Purpose and Benefits of Using the Six Thinking Hats

> *'Operacy is the skill of thinking for action instead of for description.'*
> Dr Edward de Bono

The Six Thinking Hats is a proven technique that focuses on separating out and strengthening six modes of thinking to improve individual or group consideration of ideas, problem solving and decision-making. Each thinking mode is identified with a coloured symbolic 'thinking hat'. The metaphor of wearing and switching 'hats' is a means to focus on or redirect thoughts and conversations. It provides a framework to help learners think clearly and thoroughly by directing their attention in one direction at a time (parallel thinking): the white hat concerns facts; the green hat creativity; the yellow hat benefits; the black hat risks; the red hat feelings; and the blue hat processes.

The Six Thinking Hats is a system to teach, promote and nurture thinking. It will benefit any learning environment and result in young people who enjoy being more independently productive, effective and creative. It is an inclusive model, meaning learners who have previously struggled to access and develop their thinking due to literacy and numeracy challenges can excel and contribute. Every child deserves to leave school with a rich, conscious repertoire of thinking tools.

The Six Thinking Hats is not subject specific so these tools will not become outdated due to changes in curriculum, context, life or work.

This is a practical, self-directing tool kit that provides clarity and space to analyse, reflect on and expand thought processes in a purposeful way. It develops good mental habits that lead to action and helps learners to overcome the following fundamental difficulties when thinking:

- **Emotion-dominated thinking** can result in us taking an immediate position based on how we feel. We then use our intelligence to support that judgement and attack the alternative point of view. The risk is we only take a narrow perspective based on gut feeling. The red hat provides a way for feelings in thinking to provide a valuable contribution but not overwhelm the process.
- **Helplessness**, where we are stuck, not knowing what to do or think. This is especially important for learners of all ages who have developed habits of learned helplessness, experiencing a lack of control, contribution and motivation. This can be linked to lack of self-esteem and has significant implications for the positive mental attitude of developing youngsters.[1]
- **Confusion**, which arises when we try to do too much at once. Often, when we try to think about something, our minds go off in several different tangents simultaneously. Some modes of thinking conflict with each other, such as creativity and judgement or emotions and objectivity.

The benefits for contemporary teaching are significant. Teachers, like any craftsperson, develop their own teaching toolkits, which is often labour intensive and heavily reliant on physical resources. The Six Thinking Hats approach provides a proven method that can be used singly or as a design process, easily adaptable for any age, experience and ability. It offers structure and consistency.

---

1. Learned Helplessness: Seligman's Theory of Depression (positivepsychology.com)

The method establishes a respect for all types of thinking and sets an expectation that everybody can improve their thinking, the impact of their actions and their contribution. All viewpoints are included, even if there is contradiction. This exploration of ideas under each hat leads to more considered actions.

The Six Thinking Hats method ensures all learners discover that it is 'fun to think', empowering them to contribute to their own learning and determine the direction required.

Increasing your teaching skills through broadening your perception and that of your learners in a range of contexts is an exciting prospect. One thought may one day change the world.

'Education is not the learning of fact, but the training of the mind to think.'
Albert Einstein

1.5 The Teaching of Thinking Skills

> 'The quality of our thinking will determine the quality of our future.'
>
> Dr Edward de Bono

■ Intelligence and Thinking

Intelligent people can sometimes be poor thinkers because the way in which they carry out their thinking is inefficient. It is like having a powerful car but driving it badly: there is nothing wrong with the car, but the driver is not making the most of the car's potential.

Consider the thinking processes of two thinkers faced with a similar situation:

Thinker A:
1. This is what I think about this matter.
2. Now, I am going to prove to you that I am right.

Thinker B:
1. I want to explore the matter.
2. Here are some alternative views that are possible.
3. This is the view I prefer.
4. Now, let me explain how I reached that conclusion.

With Thinker A, the conclusion comes first, and the thinking is just a defence of that conclusion. With Thinker B, there is an exploration of the subject leading to a conclusion, which is then explained. Thinker B is open to the possibility that there is a better answer.

■ Hats and Role-Playing

Why hats? There is a traditional association between thinking and hats.

— 'Put on your thinking cap.'

A hat is simple to put on and take off. This is relevant because we need a simple language for directing and talking about thinking. We must be able to put on or take off the different coloured hats with ease. This makes it simple to request that learners start or finish using a specific mode of thinking or switch thinking modes.

Also, hats often indicate a role. Soldiers wear special helmets. Police may wear specific hats to indicate their role. In some countries, judges wear special headpieces. Graduates wear hats to indicate their achievement in studying. So, when we put on a thinking hat, we take on the role indicated by that particular hat.

The hats are not for categorising people. It is counterproductive to say, 'She's a green hat thinker', or 'He only uses the red hat'. Although these may be accurate assessments, if we start to use the hats to label people, then we box in their potential. This is the opposite of the purpose of the Six Thinking Hats method, which is to encourage people to use all six modes of thinking.

Using physical hats is fun and visually supportive for many learners. It is essential for teachers to direct the thinking deliberately and for all thinkers to use the specifically requested mode of thinking symbolised by the choice of hat, at the same time, in parallel: 'When I put on this colour hat (pick up this flag, hold this coloured square, step in this coloured circle, sit on this coloured beanbag, etc.), I do this kind of thinking. And when I change colours, I change to a new kind of thinking'.

Beyond Argument

Normally, if we think an idea is not workable, we will spend all of our time arguing against it. With the Six Thinking Hats method, we can learn to put on the yellow hat. In doing so, we now show that even though the idea seems useless, some good may be found in it.

Instead of saying, 'This is what I think, and I know I am right', we can learn to say, 'If you want me to play the hat roles, I can do that very well'.

We can develop a pride in the skill of carrying out the different thinking roles. As a result, our thinking about any matter will become more comprehensive and objective.

With the Six Thinking Hats method, if we do not like a suggestion, we know that there will always be a chance to check that idea with the black hat and to express our feelings with the red hat. Meanwhile, it will be possible to explore the idea with the white, yellow and green hats. Then summarise and conclude using the blue hat.

Teaching Thinking

Thinking is a skill that can be developed, regardless of age, ability and current experience, to help learners find and develop their unique voice. It improves a range of other skills, such as confident communication and expression, listening and response, empathy, curiosity, independent thought and collaboration.

However, we often misapply our thinking and fail to improve a situation. All too often, our thinking is confused and ineffective. Thus, the aim of any structured approach to teaching thinking is to develop the following skills:

- **Fluency of thinking**, where thinkers develop the ability to generate multiple ideas, thoughts and actions. The more fluent the thinking, the greater the thinker's self-image and self-efficacy. We strive for communities that direct their thinking and think freely within a climate of non-judgement and purpose.
- **Flexibility of thinking about a range of categories of ideas (or concepts)**, where learners **respond**, take greater control of their environment and extend their resourcefulness. The more adaptive the thinker, the greater their range.
- **Originality in thinking,** where learners enter a possibility system that results in original ideas and action that benefits and has value, not difference for the sake of difference.

1. The Purpose of the Hats

Developing the Learner as a Thinker

Dr John Edwards and Sandra Russell devoted many years to teaching Dr de Bono's methods to children. In 'Thinking Lessons: Points of View',[1] they emphasise, 'Children need a strong inner core of who they are. Caring about what others think is important, and it can also lead to discounting your own ideas. Many children learn over time to downplay their own voice, to be fearful, conservative, and 'convenient'. This tool kit aims to help children find and celebrate their unique voice, and at the same time to know how to collaborate strongly with others to learn together '.

The direct teaching of thinking will nurture learners' self-worth and promote curiosity, increased independence and open-mindedness, all through scaffolded exploration. How will you know this is working in the classroom, in the home and in daily life so that you become fellow travellers on the thinking journey?

As they develop their own 'unique voice' learners will apply it in their play, in their learning both in and out of school, and in conversation with their families and friends. Coping with uncertainty, free from the idea that an idea or situation is simply right or wrong, and demonstrating the courage to create alternatives will evidence increased belief in themselves as thinkers. They will act like thinkers and encourage thinking in others.

They will be responsive, working well within an environment that encourages appropriate pace and fluency of thinking. They will apply their thinking in a range of scenarios as well as to topical issues that they find relevant to their fast-paced and complex worlds. They will enjoy thinking.

They will identify facts, express their feelings, generate possibilities, evaluate positives, share risks and, most importantly, organise their thinking constructively before taking action.

— 'What are we going to think about?'
— 'Do we need a different way of thinking about this?'
— 'How can we explore this together?'
— 'What thinking tool can we use here?'
— 'Are there other ways we can look at this?'

Learning to listen and communicate in more constructive ways will develop their 'thinking muscle'.

'Teaching is a creative profession, not a delivery system. Great teachers do pass on information, but what great teachers also do is mentor, stimulate, provoke, and engage.'

Ken Robinson

---

1. See https://www.debono.com/de-bono-thinking-lessons-1/The-role-of-the-teacher

1.6
The Role of the Teacher

> 'Many people ask me if there is an "ideal" type of thinking that can be used for all occasions. The answer is that there is not.'
>
> Dr Edward de Bono,
> *Teach Your Child How to Think*

▬ Four Uses of the Hats in the Classroom

1. **Put the hat on.** We can ask a learner in a discussion to put on a particular colour hat, or we can ask a whole group to use the same colour hat for a few minutes.

   — 'I want you to give me some black hat thinking on this idea. What could go wrong?'
   — 'We're stuck. Please put on your green hat and suggest some solutions to this problem?'
   — 'What are the facts? What do we know? Time for some white hat thinking.'

2. **Take the hat off.** We can ask someone, or a group, to take off a particular hat that they seem to be using. In doing so, we are asking the learner to move away from that type of thinking. The Six Thinking Hats system provides a non-critical method for this.

   — 'That's red hat thinking. Please take off your red hat for a moment.'
   — 'You have given us good black hat thinking. Now please take off your black hat.'
   — 'You've thought of lots of new ideas and possibilities. I think we should take off our green hats now.'

3. **Switch hats.** Once the rules have been established, we can ask for an instant switch in thinking by suggesting that a learner take off one hat and put on another. This avoids offending the learner, as we are not attacking the thinking that is taking place but asking for a change.

   — 'We've heard good things. Now let's switch from the yellow hat to the black hat. Where might we run into trouble if we do it this way?'
   — 'With your black hat, you've done a good job of telling us why this idea might not work. Now let's switch to the green hat to see if we can fix these problems.'
   — 'That's an interesting idea. Now let's take off our green hats and put on our white hats. For now, let's talk only about the facts.'

4. **Signal thinking.** We can name a hat to show the type of thinking that we are going to use. For instance, if there is a need to discuss challenges to an idea without giving offense to an individual, putting on the black hat makes it possible.. Use the hats yourself, teaching the hats as you go.

   — ''Putting on my black hat, I'm thinking that it won't work to get out the musical instruments now because we won't have enough time to put them away before lunch.'
   — 'Putting on my red hat for a moment, I have to say that I just do not like the idea of using those shelves for the science books. I'm not sure why.'
   — ''Putting on my green hat, I want to tell you a new idea I thought of for those of you who are working on the computer today.'

In summary, we can ask learners to put on, take off, switch or signal hats. We can also put on or take off a hat ourselves. The structure and 'game' aspect of the method is one of its greatest virtues. It is important to use the language of coloured hats. It is this that allows an instant switch of thinking – as deliberate as changing gears on a bicycle.

The Influential Adult

All adults who influence the younger generation are teachers. In schools, the expectation is that they provide a rich and often bespoke learning experience. They foster curiosity, a love of learning and self-belief so that a child will strive with developing confidence to reach their potential. Schools are amazing places – centres of learning, socialisation and compassion, where conversation and new ideas can be shared and explored. But then, so are homes. Most of a child's time, as much as 85%, is spent outside of the school environment. Families share in the development, and so the following chapters have been written with a collaboration between schools and families in mind.

In the previous chapter, we considered the value of teaching thinking as a discrete skill and started to explore the impact that this approach might have on young people's success. In this chapter, we focus on that which is within your control: your enthusiasm, commitment and confidence and the way in which you plan your environment so that thinking for independence and purposeful action becomes the expectation. Teachers ensure that the challenge posed for learners is underpinned by a robust culture of well-being. The teacher's well-being is seen as a prerequisite for the well-being of learners and where the culture is one of thriving. Mistakes are celebrated as part of the learning process, and decision-making, self-expression and fearless contribution are rewarded.

Consider the following questions: what is your experience of thinking? What impact have thinking tools had on your life and work and from what age? How confident are you in your own passion and commitment to continually improving your own thinking repertoire? When was the last time you thought deeply about something and were able to share your views in a structured and successful way?

The art of teaching requires those who undertake it to enjoy the process of learning, whether as a teacher in the classroom, a coach on the football pitch or a granddad building a model Formula 1 circuit with his three-year-old grandson, channelling thinking by routinely asking, 'What are you thinking now? What shall we do next? What if? Through nurturing their own 'learning muscles', teachers adapt to the context and experience of their learning community. They teach to think by providing opportunities to create a 'beautiful mind'.

In schools, teachers develop alongside the staff and children they work closely with and effectively model their practice of thinking, demonstrating the responsive nature of the process as well as being explicit in the need to avoid confusion. Teachers are vigilant, actively listening and observing the learners as they apply their thinking skills. They use this knowledge to shape future discussions and promote the transference of skills along the concrete-to-abstract continuum – from 'what is' to 'what could be'.

Inspirational teachers are adept in using their tools to develop interest, curiosity, understanding and clarity. They inspire other adults and learners to think effectively. Teachers plan carefully so that each session has a clear-thinking process that is effectively paced and flows well. They also notice when intervention is required because the discussion topic overshadows the thinking tool. As learners experience flow, they will will become more comfortable offering their thoughts.

Sessions are pitched accurately, understanding the learners' experience, language and communication levels, and cognitive ability. This is the key in the design process.

1. The Purpose of the Hats

The teacher is the designer and conductor of the sessions. They understand the learners' current knowledge of the thinking process and the planned scenario. Scenarios can be wide ranging. Draw on your ideas and experience and that of your learners.

Teachers observe learners during the thinking process and facilitate a cognitive meta-language. You will see that each of the following chapters provides the opportunity to develop this language through the single hat guidance and then the system approach in a simple and meaningful way.

As Mick Waters says in his work Thinking Allowed: On Schooling: 'We are surely not expecting finished human beings at school leaving age. Is it not more realistic to expect that when they leave, they are primed for the future - ready to move forward with confidence, curiosity and commitment'. This is where it begins.

The Enabling Environment

What might you see, hear and experience in an environment equipped to develop thinking skills? Perhaps engagement, enjoyment, humour, active listening, respect, curiosity, idea generation and process focus, along with emotion, positivity, caution and discovery. All are welcome here, and all are descriptors of a thinking skills classroom. An environment where all learners, regardless of age, are free to enjoy exploration and challenge. Play is important for learners to understand as it builds confidence in thinking.

'Play is a very misused adult word. To a child it is a way of life. To an adult it often means unimportant recreational things we do when we are not working.'

Jean Jaques Rousseau

Through exploring their world, learners who use a range of thinking skills benefit from each other. They look for connections and promote their ideas. Constructive environments give them the courage and capacity to stretch themselves and celebrate. Environments are successful when there is deliberate, regular and routine practice that is planned progressively and acknowledges the developing sophistication. Visual prompts and ongoing opportunities for effective application of thinking reinforce and evolve the learning. Working walls provide clues and references explicitly linked to thinking and promote interactive contribution from all learners. What might your thinkers benefit from, and how might this help them develop independence and application of their developing thinking?

How will you provide a developing sense of 'I wonder' 'That's interesting' 'Mmmm I am going to have to think about that'. Where the well-being is protected and promoted through a developing sense of awe, the feeling that they are engaging in activity that is larger than themselves. This leads to feelings of contribution, connection and gratitude. Teachers use a range of strategies to motivate, include and advance thinking. This requires expert adaptation for learners experiencing a range of specific needs and is best planned by the adults who know them best. Supporting adults must modify the teaching for those learners who require additional processing time, have specific social and emotional needs, and may not be able to access the sessions routinely. All influencing adults should facilitate effectively, know their learners well and support them to access the thinking sessions confidently, so they can reduce their reliance on adults. Teaches create a culture of risk taking and the ability to cope with not knowing.

When learning is collaborative, learners can support each other and make their thinking clear through discussion. Regular dialogue around the application and function of the Six Thinking Hats tool is crucial to developing confident, skilled thinkers. Regular exemplification of the modes of thinking that follow seeks to engage and stimulate the thinking process. This enables abstract thought to become concrete by linking thought to action. Learners as thinkers transfer the thinking skills taught and learned, using them as often as possible and in different environments. Teachers can use them with the staff in their team to promote a thinking culture.

In Teach Your Child How to Think, Dr Edward de Bono clearly states, 'At the end of your thinking you should have a better map of what you have been thinking about. If nothing else, you have gone over the territory. You have explored.' The following chapters concern the ways in which to explore.

> 'Children should be taught how to think, not what to think.'
>
> Margaret Mead

References

- *Thinking Allowed: on Schooling* – Waters, Mick
- *Dialogic Teaching* – Alexander, Robin
- *Awe: The Transformative Power of Everyday Wonder* – Keltner, Prof. Dacher
- *Children Solve Problems* – de Bono, Dr Edward
- *Teach Your Child How To Think* – de Bono, Dr Edward
- *How To Have A Beautiful Mind* – de Bono, Dr Edward
- The value of teaching thinking, It is a human right to think. Metacognition and self-regulation | EEF (educationendowmentfoundation.org.uk)

1.7
A Model Lesson Plan

> *'The need to be right all the time is the biggest bar to new ideas.'*
> Dr Edward de Bono

■ Single Hat and Sequence Use

The hats can be used singly at any point in thinking and for directing and switching thinking. There is a lesson for each of the hats in section 2.

As understanding and skill improve, short sequences of two or three hats may be used together for a particular purpose. For example, the yellow hat followed by the black hat may be used to assess an idea. The black hat followed by the green hat may be used to improve a design (i.e. to point out the faults and overcome them). A longer sequence of hats may be used as a framework for thinking about a subject. This framework is set up in advance as a programme for thinking – a thinking agenda. The thinkers then follow the steps of that programme. There are lessons on building and using sequences of hats in section 3.

■ Handling Overlap

Sessions introducing the hats should move briskly, and discussion should be as practical as possible. As each hat is taught, give repeated clear examples of its uses.

Matters will arise which can be confusing. For example, many ideas may fit under two hats simultaneously. There needn't be any problem with this – simply identify how you are deciding to accept and make use of the comment.

Learner: "That's not green hat; that's yellow!"

Teacher: "Perhaps it's both because it's stating something good about the situation but also offers a new suggestion. Let's include it on our list under the green hat because we're trying to think of new ideas at the moment."

If the comment is clearly off target, settle the matter quickly and move on.

Learner: "I think that's a good plan."

Teacher: "Your comment is okay for red hat thinking, but we're using the yellow hat right now. What are the good points about the plan? Why do you think it's good?"

■ The Purpose of and the Plan for Single Hat Use

The purpose of the sessions is to direct attention to the thinking process. This can only happen if there is sufficient variation in the scenarios so that no single topic occupies too much time and learners are forced to shift their attention across a range of topics. This point is fundamental. If the lesson becomes a discussion of the content, it may be fascinating, but it becomes useless as a thinking lesson.

Each thinking hat chapter contains a session plan with additional scenarios to support the application of thinking required, helping learners to co-construct ideas and investigate further. Once familiar with the approach, an inspired and informed teacher will want to create their own scenarios. Ideas can be directly relevant to a learner's experience or deliberately removed so that a learner can practise thinking rather than knowledge retrieval.

Key Learning Points

What follows is a set of key teaching points that will support learners to think more effectively across all thinking hat sessions. You will find key learning points relevant to the specific hats within the relevant chapters.

- Carefully consider the learners' resilience, cognitive development, and age. This will have an impact on how you organise the session.
- It is expected that the adult or adults working with the learners should have secure knowledge of the learners' current confidence and competence as well as of the Six Thinking Hats system and will adapt the teaching to serve the thinking.
- Prior to any thinking session, any pre-requisite learning or information the adults or learners lack and need to be prepared for should be addressed. This will aid the flow of the session and the impact of the learning.
- Teachers must remain in the correct mode of thinking throughout the session and acknowledge any misconceptions. The role modelling and accurate directing of thinking are crucial to the learners' development.
- Avoid confusion at all costs. If there is confusion, seek to simplify things. Offer clear examples.
- The teaching must be clearly focused on the mode of thinking that is being taught. Make a point of repeating the name of the hat as often as possible where appropriate.
- The pace must be brisk. Keep the practice items short and the feedback fast. Then, move on to the next one. You will no doubt develop your own scenarios as you become inspired.
- The learning and practice must be enjoyable. Enjoyment arises from active use of the thinking skill, lively practice items and imaginative answers to stimulate learners. If a topic does not work well, move on to another.

Structure

There are six stages for each 45-minute session, as follows: **Lead in, Explanation and Demonstration, Practice, Elaboration** and **Conclusion.** An assessment using the six hats framework is provided after the lesson.

1. The Purpose of the Hats

Model Session

LEAD-IN (5 minutes)	Ask learners to talk with a partner and remind them of the purpose and benefit of any previous hats taught. If other hats have been introduced, review the learning. Learners could describe where they have applied the skill.

1. Encourage learners to remind each other about what is unique to those hats.
2. Learners should describe to their partner/s whether, and where, they used or witnessed this thinking during the week.
3. Invite queries and feedback on examples and address any misconceptions.

When moving on to a new hat, start with a story, activity or simple illustration which exemplifies the desired mode of thinking.

EXPLANATION AND DEMONSTRATION
(10 minutes)

1. Guide learners through the first scenario presented in the model plan found in the chapter you have chosen or create a scenario of your own. Check for accuracy in the learners' understanding.
2. Request feedback on the previous activity. Invite learners to describe the characteristics and purpose of the specific hat.
3. Address any misconceptions about the hat, highlight the correct thinking mode, and explain the hat's purpose and benefit. As with any previous hats, it is important to keep repeating and emphasising the hat. Contrast it with the other hats. For example, the white hat (information) is for assembling cooking ingredients, while the black and yellow hats are for tasting (evaluating) what has been cooked. This reinforces the unique purpose of each hat.
4. Exemplify each hat's language and mode of thinking from the outset. For example: 'This is white hat thinking.' 'Let's all put on our red hats.' 'We need some black hat thinking here.' 'Are we all ready to put on our green hat? We need alternatives.' 'Let's summarise our discussion and plan the next action – blue hats to the ready.'
5. Offer another interesting example, demonstrating the process in use. Invite discussion, suggestions and questions.

PRACTICE
(15 minutes)

– This is the most important part of the teaching: the learners themselves use the process on practice items.
– The practice items cover a range of ages and abilities, so choose those most appropriate to the group. A quick pace is crucial so that learners apply the desired thinking to a range of scenarios. Teaching the thinking skill is the priority, so do not become attached to any one scenario, as it is not the point of the lesson. Invite feedback on how the thinking was applied. If you have groups, then ask for one suggestion from each group.
– Learners should collaborate in groups of four or five on the activities. Provide a time frame for each exercise. After the time is up, invite learners to share their thinking.
– Guide the focus towards the required thinking skill. Invite feedback on the skill's application. If you have groups, then ask for one suggestion from each group.
– As learners become fluent thinkers you might want to identify an observer who focuses on how well the group uses the specific thinking skill and then provides feedback to the group.
– Make a range of scenarios accessible for independent practice.

deBono THE SIX THINKING HATS FOR SCHOOLS AND FAMILIES®

ELABORATION (5 minutes)	This stage provides further opportunity for learners to observe, reflect, and ask and answer questions. It could also be an opportunity to identify where the thinking skill might be useful outside of the classroom. Over time, fluent use of the hats will develop, with learners leading their own thinking.
CONCLUSION (5 minutes)	Summarise the main points, emphasising why the process can be useful. Invite discussion on the thinking technique, not the content. Use the learning points given in each chapter to discuss the use of the tool. As fluency increases and flow occurs, you may want to introduce stretch and challenge.
ASSESSMENT AND EVALUATION AFTER THE LESSON (5 minutes)	🔵 How would you summarise the outcome of the session? 🔴 How do you feel the session went? 🟡 What went well during the session? ⚫ What needs strengthening? ⚪ What facts support this evaluation? ⚪ What could you add so that your session works for all thinkers? 🟢 What could you do differently next time? 🔵 What actions will you take for next time?

▬ Resources

The key resource is the mind of the learner. The purpose of the sessions is to develop thinking as a directed skill that learners can apply to any situation. The purpose is not to have a discussion around the scenarios. Learners do not need to absorb additional facts before they start thinking, meaning those who struggle to absorb facts will find that they enjoy the thinking sessions.

There are a variety of scenarios available to support your planning and inspire further ideas. Modify, adapt and add to them to suit your context. They should engage learners to such a degree that they make thinking worthwhile and enjoyable.

The teaching of thinking skills can be related to a range of situations, applied to matters of significance or enjoyed as a moment of fun. Scenarios that are removed from reality provide thinking space that suffers less from established experience and emotions, while purposeful and familiar situations often inspire greater depth. Balancing these is the key to success. It is important to provide a variety of opportunities to practise the thinking skill.

2 *Learning the Hats*

Effective thinking requires an information base. However, it is unrealistic to assume that we will collect enough information to do our thinking for us. Only in very rare instances can we ever have such complete information about a subject that thinking is superfluous. In most cases, we must supplement inadequate information with our thinking skills.

2.1
White Hat Summary

The White Hat is for facts and the request for information.

All facts are welcome, even if they are in conflict with each other.

'The analysis of data will not by itself produce new ideas.'

Dr Edward de Bono

Your Notes

Description of the White Hat

The white hat requires information gathering, retrieval and validation. It is neutral, objective and detached. It directs attention towards established knowledge as well as information that may be missing – visualise a blank sheet of paper or computer screen. Reporting what you know someone else thinks or feels is also white hat thinking; however, reporting your own opinions or feelings is purely red hat thinking.

We can visualise ourselves as explorers wearing the white hat to make a map. We fill in the areas which are known and identify the areas for which more information is needed.

Purpose of White Hat Thinking

The white hat allows thinkers to seek and check facts in parallel. Without an initial body of information, there is no thinking. There is a specific focus on information, statistics, facts and the reported beliefs and opinions of others. All facts are welcome, even if they conflict with each other.

The session is free from one's own opinion, judgement, emotion or creative intervention. If someone offers their own opinion, judgement, feeling or new idea, thank them for their input and explain that you are looking for white hat thinking.

Using the white hat in the initial stages of a thinking session is useful. As thinking develops, it can be used to check for relevance and validity and to identify any gaps before any conclusions are drawn or actions taken.

White Hat Questioning

- What information do we have?
- What information do we need? What is missing?
- How do we find out the information that we need?
- When searching for information digitally, what implications might we need to consider?
- Jake, if you were wearing the white hat, what might you say?

While looking at the information that you have, ask further questions:
- What information is most important?
- How valid/up to date is this information?
- What is most relevant to what we are trying to achieve?
- When will we know we have sufficient information?
- When does a feeling become a fact?

Skills Developed

Skills developed include disciplined thinking, assessment, objectivity, listening for information, responsive questioning, filtering and validating sources, locating and accessing relevant information, prioritisation and organisation.

Validity and Contradiction

The white hat can be used to check for validity and confirm sources and accuracy. If there is contradictory information or a disagreement about validity or relevance, then this should be noted under the white hat but not yet resolved. Determining the validity of information is a matter for black hat thinking: checking evidence and logic and so forth. This black hat challenge is not carried out during the white hat thinking. In summary:

1. Note the challenge and return to it later with specific black hat thinking.
2. Note any disagreement or doubt so that it becomes part of the information.
3. Jot down the original and the contradictory information so that both versions are available. If the issue becomes important later, both can be checked out. For example, if someone claims that an important date was 10 December and someone else claims it was 8 December, record both versions and then get on with the white hat thinking.

In this way, the flow of white hat thinking continues. If there is constant switching between the white and black hats, the process becomes messy. So, proceed to make the map, but put question marks where needed.

▬ Key White Hat Learning Points

- Identifies conflicting information and records both points in parallel.
- Assesses information for accuracy, relevance and validity.
- Keeps it simple and does not confuse facts with judgements or possibilities or start with an opinion that drives biased thinking.
- Understands that others' known feelings can be recorded – it is a fact that someone feels a certain way.
- Remains vigilant to any important information that may be missing. There may be knowledge gaps that need to be addressed. Effective questioning helps identify what that information is and where it may be found.

▬ Example White Hat Scenarios (Additional topics in section 4)

YOUNGER LEARNERS	OLDER LEARNERS

LEAD-IN (5 minutes)

Guess My Favourite Space

Introduce the session with a short visualisation script and talk learners through your favourite space, identifying key facts about it so that they can see it clearly. Encourage learners to 'notice what they notice'.

Ask learners to communicate five facts about their favourite space. What information might they include so that their partner can guess where it is? If it is a beach or a park, which one specifically? The better the facts, the easier to guess, which is the point.

Potential Responses
- I pass this space each day on my walk to school.
- It is part of an outdoor space, with a lake and a garden centre.
- The area I am in has a sign at the entrance that says, 'Suitable access for all'.
- It is a wooded area with children's size picnic benches.

First Impressions

Explain to the learners that a famous art critic is coming to view their exhibition. What information might be useful to include in their 'gallery'? Who else might they ask to support preparations?

Potential Responses
- I would describe the inspiration for my art, for example, the local landscape, climate change or love.
- I need to provide background information that tells the story of the pieces exhibited and the media used, with dated examples of the artistic portfolio that demonstrate the work's journey/evolution.
- I can visit a local gallery, invite a local gallery owner or artist to my gallery, or perform online research to identify any information I may have missed.

26 | THE SIX THINKING HATS FOR SCHOOLS AND FAMILIES® deBono

2. Learning the Hats   The White Hat

Younger Learners   Older Learners

EXPLANATION AND DEMONSTRATION *(10 minutes)*

Our Garden

The local garden centre has agreed to donate plants to the class garden. What information do you need to consider so that you choose your plants wisely?

Potential Responses
- Our survey has identified that most people want a mixture of flowering plants and vegetables.
- We have three raised beds and a border area to fill.
- Mr Jukes is overseeing the project because he knows a lot about gardening. We can check any concerns or questions with him.

Getting the Job Done

The group are preparing for their first work experience and need to write an application to the company. What five key things should they know about the company to increase their chance of success?

Potential Responses
- Is the company working in an area that inspires/excites me? What information has any research given me so far?
- What skills is this company looking for in potential employees? What is missing from my application, and how can I demonstrate I have the skills?

PRACTICE *(15 minutes)*

A Dog's Life!

Your family are looking after a friend's dog while the friend is on holiday. What questions will you need to ask before the dog arrives?

Potential Responses
- I would ask about the dog's eating and sleeping routines.
- We need to know whether the dog likes a bath and, if so, what the usual routine is.
- What is the dog like on a lead? Does the dog enjoy a walk, does he like other dogs, and will he come back if I call him?

Holiday Escapades

Your parents have decided to go on their first camping holiday abroad. So that the whole family have an enjoyable time, what information might you need to know as part of the plan?

Potential Responses
- What equipment will we need to consider so that we are as comfortable as possible? What sized tent do we need? What will we sleep on? What will we eat?
- Where are we intending to go?
- Who do we know who has been camping before and could answer some of our questions or advise us on what might be missing?

2. Learning the Hats   The White Hat

Younger Learners & Older Learners

ELABORATION
(5 minutes)

Encouraging reflective practice to answer the following questions:
- What did they notice?
- What went well?
- What challenges did they face when using the thinking skills?
- How could they improve their white hat thinking?
- Where will they use this type of thinking in their life?

Teacher modelling is useful too. It is crucial that learners witness adults applying, talking through and explaining their authentic use of the hats. Over time, fluent use of the hats will develop, with learners leading their own thinking and observing that of others.

Help the learners distinguish between facts and other kinds of points, such as feelings, opinions and suggestions. For instance, 'I love the view from our windows' (red hat) could be reworded to make it a neutral point: 'The room has windows with a view of the front lawn'. 'The room is crowded' (black hat) could be rephrased to say, 'The desks and bookcases take up most of the floor space'.

CONCLUSION
(5 minutes)

- Summarise the main points of the session.
- Describe how white hat thinking enables you to map known information and identify missing information.
- Reflect on the thinking skill explored and developed in the session.
- Use the key questions and learning points given in the chapter to discuss the use of the tool. As fluency increases and flow occurs, you may want to introduce stretch and challenge into your sessions.

WHITE HAT DIALOGUE

'I love white hat thinking – it's just facts, facts and more facts.'
'Thank you for that information. How do we know that is a fact?'
'Thank you for that description; let's all think about that. Has anybody got any more information to add?'
'My mind is like a computer.'
'He said he was eight years old and loved playing hockey'.
'I just know something is missing.'

Next Hat: Red Hat

'If you are tuned out of your own emotions, you will be poor at reading them in other people.'

Daniel Goldman,
author, psychologist and science journalist

2.2
Red Hat Summary

The red hat is for feelings.

No justification or explanation is allowed.

'It is not the logical part of thinking that changes emotions but the perceptual part of it. If we see something differently, our emotions may alter with the altered perceptions.'

Dr Edward de Bono

Your Notes

2. Learning the Hats The Red Hat

Description of the Red Hat

The red hat represents emotions, feelings and instincts. Visualise a red heart emoji – think of anger and joy but also of warmth and contentment. The red hat includes both intense and gentle feelings. When you are engaged in this type of thinking, you can express your feelings and instincts, but you must not justify or defend them with logic. The red hat provides the space to say, 'This is how I feel about the situation'. Equally, it provides other people with the opportunity to share their feelings, too, and these become valid inputs to the thinking process. The awareness of how we feel about a situation helps explain why we think the way we do and discover where there are opportunities to broaden that thinking with other hats at a later stage. For example, if you dislike an idea, it may be useful to explore the yellow hat (positive aspects).

Purpose of Red Hat Thinking

Emotions and intuition play an important part in thinking but are culturally considered less valuable than logic. We therefore make the mistake of disguising our feelings as logic when we cannot explain or justify them. We are then committed to supporting that rationalisation. The purpose of the red hat is to separate out emotions and feelings from logic (the yellow and black hats) and facts (the white hat). Emotions and intuition are closely tied to our values and, therefore, are an important ingredient in thinking. Red hat thinking is not right or wrong, but it has a profound influence on what happens with our thinking. It is important to understand what these influences are. Your red hat thinking can and often does change due to the use of the other hats.

We cannot put feelings to one side and pretend that thinking should always be objective and free of feeling. Without feelings, values would have little power, and without values, thinking would be inhuman. It also would be almost impossible to make choices. Used at the right place, feelings decide the value of thinking for ourselves as individuals and for society as a whole. Used at the wrong point, though, feelings can sabotage thinking. Strong feelings at the beginning of thinking (jealousy, fear, anger , etc.) so limit one's perception that thinking can only be used to support these feelings.

The value of the red hat is that it recognises feelings, emotions, hunches and intuitions as a valid part of thinking and simultaneously labels them for what they are.

Red Hat questioning

- How do I feel about this right now?
- What is my intuition telling me?
- What is my gut reaction to this situation?
- What am I doing when I feel at my best? What does my best feel like?

Skills Developed

Skills include expressive language use, self-reflection, increased emotional vocabulary use, empathy, care for others, self-regulation and communication.

Key Red Hat Learning points

- The expression of both positive and negative feelings is permitted during red hat sessions. This can lead to more sophisticated use of emotional language. It is the teacher's responsibility to ensure the learners' well-being prior to their exploration of emotions. Often, adults will know the learners well and

2. Learning the Hats The Red Hat

understand when there may be emotional triggers that can disrupt or deregulate them. Providing a safe environment wherein all staff ensure that trust and security are built on daily is essential for this activity.

- Emotions are a necessary part of the thinking process. There are two key reasons to use this mode of thinking: to elicit feelings and make them known and to make assessments or choices.
- It is crucial not to justify or explain red hat thinking, even if you are able to do so. This ensures that the red hat is separated from the logical (yellow and black) and objective (white) hats. Also, we cannot always justify our emotions and intuition. A lack of justification does not make the red hat less influential for the person who feels a certain way.
- The red hat makes feelings legitimate. Do not apologise by saying things such as, 'It is only a feeling'.
- The red hat does not give people permission to be offensive or insulting. We just say what we feel. We do not accuse others of anything (i.e. 'I feel angry', not 'I feel that you are stupid').
- The red hat can be used at the beginning of a thinking session, as well as prior to or just after a decision is made.

Example Red Hat Scenarios (Additional topics in section 4)

YOUNGER LEARNERS | OLDER LEARNERS

LEAD-IN (5 minutes)

My Learning Space

Introduce the class teddy bear, who is wearing his red hat today. Explain that 'Teddy' has been thinking overnight about how he feels when he watches the children learn. Sometimes, he feels happy, sometimes sad, depending how involved the children are. He thinks it is time for us all to talk about how we feel in the classroom. (An extra member of staff could observe responses for staff evaluation and discussion.)

Use the teddy to demonstrate where a pupil makes a legitimate red hat comment and model an appropriate non-judgemental response.

Potential Responses
- The best bit is outdoors. It is exciting whizzing around on the bikes.
- The quiet area is lovely. I feel very peaceful and think about my mom when I am sitting there.
- The construction area is boring; there is not enough for us to do.

Inside Out

The school has successfully acquired funding to develop the outdoor learning environment. There is a list of criteria it needs to follow to secure the funding. The improvement needs to do the following:

- Increase learners' motivation.
- Regardless of age, help all learners stay healthy.
- Ensure there is a safe space for children when they need it.
- Be beautiful and encourage the presence of wildlife.

Using a range of resources, discuss the environment they currently access. This could be viewing photographs or a simple video or taking a learning walk.

Use large sheets of paper to record words or images to gather the children's collective thoughts.

- How do learners feel when they learn outdoors now?
- If they could change three things, what would they be, and how would the changes make them feel?

Potential Responses
- I feel restless at lunchtime.
- I would love to see climbing walls.
- My old school has a bowling alley. I felt excited to play.

2. Learning the Hats — The Red Hat

	Younger Learners	Older Learners

EXPLANATION AND DEMONSTRATION *(10 minutes)*

Younger Learners

Poem

Choose a poem with which the children can explore feelings from the perspective of the characters. Explore the poem with the children and ask them how the characters might be feeling in each verse. The learners can develop their own expressive language through exploration of the language within the poem.

Older Learners

Make yourself at home

A family is about to host a Spanish exchange student. They are keen to ensure that their visitor feels welcome and 'at home'. They decide to engage in a discussion so that everyone in the family can express their thoughts about the impending visit and the change to routine.

Potential Responses
– I feel strongly that we need to give them their own space and make it feel a bit like their space at home.
– I wouldn't be happy if I had to give up my room.
– I am curious to find out what they like to do. It will be fun to show them the sights.
– I feel a bit irritated having a stranger in the house. What if I can't understand them?

PRACTICE *(15 minutes)*

Younger Learners

Our World

As part of a project to appreciate the local environment, teachers have asked families to encourage the skill of observing wildlife during a walk, cycle or scoot. To prepare children for this activity, ask them to close their eyes and quietly imagine how they would feel about a world without birds, bees, butterflies and foxes or without flowers, trees and the plants in their gardens. Using your own context, you can help learners add to this list. To support younger learners, you may want to consider resources such as feelings cards to help them identify their emotions.

Questions to prompt feelings could include the following:
– What were you feeling about this world?
– When you are out, what creatures make you happy? Sad? Scared? Peaceful? Excited?
– How do you feel about going home and sharing a walk with your family where you try to spot as many living things as you can?

Potential Responses
– I was scared; it was too quiet.
– I was angry. I couldn't see my guinea pigs and the flowers my granddad grows. Everything felt empty.

Older Learners

In the Spotlight

The learners are going to perform a 'mini' concert for their parents. You want to understand how they feel about the idea of performing. You have a set of questions to help them formulate their red hat thinking.

– How do you feel about this idea?
– What areas promote feelings of confidence, and what areas do not?
– What feelings might the audience have?

Create a list of expectations for the performance and encourage the learners to describe how they feel about them, for example, playing an instrument, singing, performing solo or as part of a group, playing recently learned pieces or developing a new composition. (This could be extended and used as an initial survey of feelings around confidence and perceived competence.)

Potential Responses
– This is such a cool opportunity. I love performing to an audience.
– I'm not sure – I am not confident.
– I find working in a group stressful; I am much more content going solo.
– First thoughts: terrified, but still interested. I would need to know more about what I need to do to make me feel comfortable.

2. Learning the Hats — The Red Hat

	Younger Learners	Older Learners

PRACTICE (15 minutes)

Younger Learners:
- I felt very small.
- I felt very confused and thought about the creatures in the sea. I was lonely.

Older Learners:
- This is exciting.
- I am looking forward to this.
- I am worried I might make a mistake.

ELABORATION (5 minutes)

Encourage reflective practice to answer the following questions:
- What did they notice?
- What went well?
- What challenges did they face when using the thinking skills?
- How could they improve their red hat thinking?
- Where will they use this type of thinking in their life?

Teacher modelling is useful too.

CONCLUSION (5 minutes)

- Summarise the main points of the session.
- Describe how red hat thinking enables you to express what you feel or perceive without justification.
- Reflect on the thinking skill explored and developed in the session.

RED HAT DIALOGUE

'I'm scared of falling. Will you hold my hand?'
'You mean we can say anything we feel?'
'Thank you for letting us know how you feel about the visit.'
'I don't really like working in a group. Other people think and speak quickly and make me feel very confused.'
'I am not too sure about that idea.'
'I want to put on my red hat please... I am very pleased with my group today.'
Science experiments are my very favourite thing to do. I love solving problems and asking, 'What if'.
'That is so out of order.'
'I feel that you are bullying me.'

■ **Next Hat: Black Hat**

'A person who dare not admit he is wrong inflates his ego but weakens his self.'

Dr Edward de Bono

2.3
Black Hat Summary

The black hat is for caution.

What are the risks and issues?
What are the faults or weaknesses?

The black hat is important, powerful and essential. It is not a bad hat – rather, it is overuse of the black hat that is bad.

A logical justification must be given.

'Everyone has the right to doubt everything as often as he pleases and the duty to do it at least once. No way of looking at things is too sacred to be reconsidered. No way of doing things is beyond improvement.'

Dr Edward de Bono

Your Notes

Description of the Black Hat

The black hat is for critical thinking. The word critical originally comes from the Greek word to judge (*kritikos*); in many countries, lawyers and judges wear black robes in court. Using the black hat protects us from making dangerous or unworkable decisions. With the black hat, we find weaknesses and flaws and predict problems that may arise. The black hat is an important and powerful hat. It represents caution and helps us to identify risks. It is not enough to state the issue – you also have to explain why it is a problem. This involves assessing to check the feasibility of an idea or proposal. Identifying issues is a crucial step towards finding potential resolutions that can be generated later using the green hat. The black hat is vital but often overused. That does not mean that it is a 'bad' hat; rather, it is the overuse that is probelmatic. A small amount of salt improves a meal, but too much will ruin it. Encourage thinkers to justify their black hat statements, drawing out the appropriate thinking approach and addressing any misconceptions sensitively and wisely. This will reinforce the crucial nature of this mode of thinking.

Purpose of Black Hat Thinking

The two main purposes of black hat thinking are to find and evaluate weaknesses and make constructive assessments of a situation or idea based on sound judgement. The purpose of the black hat is not to attack but to examine an idea or situation. The black hat usefully identifies when an idea does not align with our expectations. This stops us from making mistakes. The black hat provides an opportunity for all involved to apply caution and not to get sidetracked by positive or creative thinking. There might also be a temptation to revert to argument and continue to 'prove your point' instead of mapping the problems, obstacles, difficulties and dangers sufficiently.

In practice, there is a big difference between looking at an idea to attack or reject it and looking at an idea to improve it.

Suppose we are presented with a design for a new chair. We look for the weaknesses in the design: the seat is too small, the back is too straight, etc. Our intention may be to reject the design because of these weaknesses.

Alternatively, our intention may be to improve the design by pointing out the weaknesses so that they can be overcome , making the design stronger. This is a constructive function of the black hat. When the black hat is used this way, it is generally followed by a green hat search for ways to overcome the weaknesses. This is constructive criticism.

Overuse

The black hat is possibly the most valuable hat, but it can be overused. There are people who want to use only this hat and criticise ideas. They feel that this is enough – but it is not.

We need critical thinking, but we also need thinking that is creative, generative and productive. Where are the ideas and suggestions going to come from? Criticising ideas may improve them but does not produce new ideas. This is why the teaching of critical thinking by itself is insufficient.

Critical thinking and the black hat have an important role to play in thinking, but by themselves, they are not enough. This is not meant as a rejection of critical thinking but an observation that other kinds of thinking are also needed. One particular wheel on a car may be a very fine wheel, but it is not enough to carry the car alone.

Black Hat Questioning

- What problems can we potentially foresee? What is likely to go wrong in the future?
- What are the challenges we may need to overcome?
- What do we need to be cautious about?
- What are the risks involved? What is the strength of our evidence so far?

Skills Developed

Skills include critical thinking, reasoning, logic, assessment, inquiry, evidence-based thinking and responsibility.

Key Learning Points

- The black hat is a highly effective assessment tool. It is a crucial part of the design process. However, it is important to use the black hat wisely and accurately. It can be overused, resulting in excessive criticism of an idea.
- The black hat crucially checks for evidence, logic, feasibility, weakness and impact. Primarily, this mode of thinking is a way of cautious and skilful evaluation that aims to improve an idea, not attack it.
- All black hat comments need to be reasoned logically.
- Sometimes, this thinking may also be flagged as necessary when using the white hat.

Example Black Hat Scenarios (Additional topics in section 4)

	YOUNGER LEARNERS	OLDER LEARNERS
LEAD-IN (5 minutes)	**Never the Wrong Weather!** Presenting images or video clips of different weather conditions, ask pupils to comment as you choose appropriate clothing from a range of items. Make sure that you make obvious mistakes in your choice of clothing and invite the children to offer reasons for what they consider to be a wrong choice, identifying the potential problems. *Potential Responses* –If you wear a jumper on a hot day, you might get heatstroke. –That is not going to keep you warm. There is a blue sky, but it is autumn – look at the trees. –No, it isn't raining, but the roads and pathways are wet, →	**Hazard ahead** Use a visual stimulus to demonstrate a potentially hazardous situation, for example skateboarding. Use the following questions to guide pupils towards the black hat mode of thinking: –What risks might need assessing here? –What could potentially go wrong? –What is missing for you in this image? –What situations have you ever experienced where you needed this type of thinking? –How important is this type of thinking? *Potential Responses* –I am concerned that the skate park may be unsupervised or that the design doesn't meet safety standards. We can't really tell from this image. –I can't be sure, but looking at the clothing, I am not sure how aware this skater is of the need for protective gear. –Overconfidence could lead to attempting too advanced a trick. →

2. Learning the Hats The Black Hat

| Younger Learners | Older Learners |

LEAD-IN (5 minutes)

and look at the river. There has obviously been rain recently. You need waterproofs.

– I usually just go for it when I do anything risky. I might need to stop and think about what might go wrong.

EXPLANATION AND DEMONSTRATION (10 minutes)

DIY

Involve the pupils in a discussion about what they already know about keeping safe. Introduce new child-safe DIY tools, explaining that the pupils will learn how to use them. Direct them to think carefully about potential risks/dangers. Reinforce the language of being careful, safe, cautious and aware of others and the potential impact of carelessness and not paying attention.

Introduce the tools and explain how people might use them. Start by making unacceptable use explicit, with another member of staff modelling shock and asking questions of you so that pupils witness the exchange.

– What do you think might happen if we use our equipment like this?
– How should we use the equipment?

Ask for volunteers to demonstrate safe behaviour and celebrate sensible practice.

Potential Responses
– I think it is too heavy, and I might not be able to pick it up properly. It might fall on my foot.
– My aunty lets me carry her tools when she is doing repairs. She told me how to tap carefully in case I slipped or missed the nail and asked me to watch carefully. She is very sensible.
– It is that part that is the most dangerous because it is shiny and sharp.

Questions, Questions, Questions!

As part of a whole school conservation project a local trainee zoo keeper is visiting to discuss their exciting work with the pupils. Part of the pupils' follow-up work will be to produce a report, including any risk management related to the role. So that the pupils are fully engaged and informed you have asked them to create questions to understand the potential risks associated with the role.

Potential Responses
– What are the risks to you?
– What mistakes do visitors make that put them in danger?
– What are the risks for the animals?
– What are the top three mistakes made by zookeepers regarding their safety?

PRACTICE (15 minutes)

Puppy Love

The family have decided to buy a pet dog and are undecided whether to buy a puppy from a breeder or go to an animal rescue centre instead. As a family decide on the risks and challenges associated with each option.

Telling My Truth

Ask the children to imagine that teachers now have the right to use a lie detector when they are not sure whether somebody is telling the truth. In groups, the learners should share their black hat thinking on this issue.

deBono THE SIX THINKING HATS FOR SCHOOLS AND FAMILIES®

2. Learning the Hats | **The Black Hat**

	Younger Learners	Older Learners
PRACTICE (15 minutes)	*Potential Responses* – Are we sure that the breeding programme is safe? Even if they are enthusiastic, do we understand the implications of the breeding process? What health problems may arise? – If we go to a rescue centre, do we know what that puppy has gone through and whether we would have the skills as a family to deal with it? – The cost of a dog from a breeder is enormous. Can we afford it? – Do we know how often the rescue centres get puppies? Do we need to consider any alternatives?	*Potential Responses* – This is an invasion of privacy. – Is there a risk here of turning schools into police states? How can we avoid this? – There will be a decrease in trust. I do not think assuming guilt is the way forward. – There are so many risks here, especially when the research suggests the use of lie detectors is not as reliable as we might think.
ELABORATION (5 minutes)	Encourage reflective practice to answer the following questions: – What did they notice? – What went well? – What challenges did they face when using the thinking skills? – How could they improve their black hat thinking? – Where will they use this type of thinking in their life? Teacher modelling is useful too.	
CONCLUSION (5 minutes)	– Summarise the main points of the session. – Describe how black hat thinking enables you to identify your concerns and any problems or pitfalls you are envisaging. – Reflect on the thinking skill explored and developed in the session.	
BLACK HAT DIALOGUE	'Please take your black hat off for a while, Harry. We are looking for the positive here.' 'That is so not safe. He is too high and could fall and hurt himself.' 'Well, I have heard that there is a lot of bullying in school, so I, for one, do not feel safe.' 'If we put the factory at that place, then if there is an accident, toxic chemicals will flow into the town's water supply.' 'If you go to work in the kitchen with that thumb infection, you could make a lot of people ill with food poisoning.' 'This maths is too hard for me; I never get it right. I am just hopeless with numbers.' 'The trouble with that route is the roads become flooded.' 'I've been told if more of us don't choose music and art, the teachers will lose their jobs.' 'Have you seen the cost of that trip? There is no way my parents can afford that.' 'Those boat trips are not safe; nobody seems to be wearing a life jacket.'	

Next Hat: Yellow Hat

> 'Optimism is not a faith that things will automatically get better; it's a conviction that we can make things better.'
>
> Melinda Gates, philanthropist

2.4
Yellow Hat Summary

The yellow hat is about strengths, values and benefits.

A logical justification must be given.

'Being positive is a choice.'
Dr Edward de Bono

Your Notes

Description of the Yellow Hat

The yellow hat represents sunshine and looking on the bright side of things. The yellow hat is for identifying value. Thinkers concentrate on the benefits that could arise from an idea and that can be justified. The yellow hat must be logical; you must give supporting reasons. If you are merely expressing a general feeling of optimism or hope that something will work, then that is red hat thinking, which covers feelings.

Purpose of Yellow Hat Thinking

Using yellow hat thinking is a deliberate way to ensure a focus on the positive and clear identification of the value of any project, proposal or suggestion. It can be a more difficult process than using black hat thinking, as we are naturally better at pointing out why something does not fit our expectations than at seeking the value in a situation. The benefits of an idea can be hidden or evolving and thus can often be overlooked.

Yellow Hat Questioning

- What are the benefits here?
- How useful is this idea?
- What positive difference will this make?
- How feasible is it to make this happen?
- What value does this add to our work?

Skills Developed

Skills include benefit expression, communication, identification of possible solutions, simplification of ideas so that they work, opportunity creation, seeing what is possible, a positive mental attitude, resilience, gratitude, being able to face challenges positively, curiosity and the overall development of a growth mindset.

Key Learning Points

- Yellow hat thinking complements black hat tthinking – they balance each other.
- Using the yellow hat before the black hat is motivating, as you can quickly identify whether an idea or suggestion has a positive basis on which to proceed. If there are no strong yellow hat points, then there is no need to also spend time on the black hat points.
- Yellow hat thinking is forward focused and must be supported with logic and sound reasoning. It can also look to the past to learn from experience, identifying ideas that have previously worked and brought about positive change.
- Thinking positively involves a mixture of curiosity, pleasure and a desire 'to make things happen'.
- Yellow hat thinking looks for increased value or opportunity. It is a method to discuss why something would work and how a situation would be improved because of it.

2. Learning the Hats The Yellow Hat

Example Yellow Hat Scenarios (Additional topics in section 4)

| YOUNGER LEARNERS | OLDER LEARNERS |

LEAD-IN (5 minutes)

Time for Fun

Partnering with another staff member, model a conversation about your weekend, holiday or evening. Ask the pupils to take note of when each member of staff talks positively about their activities and invite them to recall examples. When the conversation is over, direct the children to talk to a friend/s about what they heard and then invite feedback. Acknowledge references to positive thinking and introduce the yellow hat, reinforcing any developing views the pupils have explored and addressing any misconceptions.

Potential Responses
- I heard Mrs Jones say that she is glad that she went for a walk with her dog as it calmed them both down.
- Yes, and the dog got to play with another dog, as well, which made him happy and gave him good exercise. I thought it was a great idea to plan regular long walks every weekend.
- I think Mrs Dale said that she was looking forward to her mom's party next weekend, as it would be a wonderful opportunity for most of the family to get together.
- I was glad that Mrs Jones suggested a Zoom call during the party so that her grandson wouldn't miss it completely and the birthday girl got to see all her family.

Service with a Smile

Ask pupils to volunteer on the reception desk for half an hour a day. Ensure they understand the required approach and improve their customer service skills. It is important to maintain the school's reputation for friendliness and support.

What five techniques or phrases might each pupil use to ensure they deal with any enquiry positively?

Potential Responses
- Smile and lean towards the visitor slightly to demonstrate you are listening actively.
- Demonstrate a willingness to be helpful : 'Good morning, how can I help you?'
- When presented with a problem, don't be defensive. Instead, find a way to look for opportunities to improve the situation : 'I am so sorry. I am not sure, but if you take a seat, I do know the right person who can answer your query.'

Alternative lead-ins
- What are the good points of being tall?
- What are the good points of being short?
- If dogs could be taught to speak, what would the benefits be?
- Someone suggests putting a large hook on the roofs of cars. What might the benefits be?

EXPLANATION AND DEMONSTRATION (10 minutes)

It's Great to be a Friend!

The learning adventure theme of 'friendship' has ended. So that the pupils engage in any future experiences positively, ask them to share what they have enjoyed most about their learning opportunities.

- What important ideas did they learn?
- What makes a good friend?
- What do they like most about their friends?
- Where do they get the best opportunities

The Interview

A group of pupils is taking part in the interviews for the new deputy headteacher. They are asked, as part of the process, to identify five strengths that they will be looking for when they interview. Using yellow hat thinking, ask the class groups to produce five positives that they think are important for a new deputy

2. Learning the Hats | The Yellow Hat

	Younger Learners	Older Learners
EXPLANATION AND DEMONSTRATION (10 minutes)	to make friends in school and at home? What are the benefits of these opportunities? – What is friendly about their learning environment?	headteacher and can be evaluated by the interviewing team. – They listen carefully and have a genuine interest in what we have to say. – They enjoy hobbies outside of school subjects so that they can bring interest to the classrooms. – They like children and have a passion for learning. – They have the courage to change their mind. – They are organised and reliable.
PRACTICE (15 minutes)	### Playground Games The school is keen to ensure positive play at break and lunchtime. Ask the children about the most positive parts of their play during the school day. *Potential Responses* – Games that involve people are fun. It is easier when there are simple rules to follow. This helps others identify whether they really want to join in. – It is useful when the sports ambassadors help fair play and encourage people who aren't sure how to play. – I like having spaces where we can just sit and chat. This means we can exercise and	### All the Way to the Top As part of the geography curriculum and to promote well-being, a trip has been organised for those interested in attempting the Three Peaks Challenge. The climb involves three mountains: Scafell Pike, the tallest mountain in England; Snowdon, the tallest in Wales, and Ben Nevis, the tallest in Scotland. To engage as many pupils as possible, teachers collaborate with their pupil planning group to identify as many benefits to participating as they can. *Potential Responses* – It provides an opportunity to challenge yourself and experience an enormous sense of achievement. – It provides a real purpose to get fit and healthy. – It shows the benefits of being prepared. – You will be part of a team and experience remote areas that very few people see. – There will be amazing views.

2. Learning the Hats | The Yellow Hat

Younger Learners & **Older Learners**

ELABORATION (5 minutes)	Encourage reflective practice to answer the following questions: –What did they notice? –What went well? –What challenges did they face when using the thinking skills? –How could they improve their yellow hat thinking? –Where will they use this type of thinking in their life? Teacher modelling is useful too.
CONCLUSION (5 minutes)	–Summarise the main points of the session. –Describe how yellow hat thinking enables you to develop a positive and constructive approach to thinking through scenarios, allowing you to probe for benefits and value. –Reflect on the thinking skill explored and developed in the session.
YELLOW HAT DIALOGUE	'That was an interesting lesson. Sharing our ideas was a useful way to learn, as I could compare my ideas with those of many other people.' 'The benefit of this approach is that it is simple and quick.' 'Running really helps me to relax and stay calm.' 'If you study science, you will be discovering and assessing what are good skills to develop.' 'That is a really good point and could help everyone achieve more. Thank you.' 'I am just a glass-half-full kind of girl, miss.' 'So just go over the benefits of that idea once more.' 'Okay, we have a full understanding of the Risks. How about some yellow hat thinking to balance that out?' I think Jamie has just slipped into red hat thinking about how he feels rather than explaining the positives, sir.'

▬ Next Hat: Green Hat

'Becoming is better than being.'
Carol Dweck, psychologist, fellow of the Association of Psychological Science,
    professor of pyschology at Stanford University and mindset expert

2.5
Green Hat Summary

The green hat is for creativity, for ideas, for alternatives.

The green hat is about possibility and 'what if'.

'There is no doubt that creativity is the most important human resource of all. Without creativity, there would be no progress and we would be forever repeating the same patterns.'

Dr Edward de Bono

▬ Your Notes

2. Learning the Hats — The Green Hat

Description of the Green Hat

The green hat represents growth. Green recalls nature, vegetation and abundance – think of branches. The green hat is concerned with generating alternatives and possibilities, new ways of thinking that add value. Green hat thinking encourages the development of ideas and going beyond what is known. It focuses on proposals, suggestions and new ideas.

Purpose of Green Hat Thinking

The green hat is about invention, modification and improvement. It is an opportunity for all involved to think creatively. Wearing the green hat places a deliberate focus on possibilities, on seeing familiar situations in new ways.

Black hat and yellow hat thinking are not enough because they are for 'reactive' thinking. We use these hats to judge or assess something that is put before us. But we can't judge or assess an idea until someone has generated it.

When we put forward an idea, it is only a possibility. Then, we proceed to develop the idea and check it out against the available information and our objectives. We bring in the yellow hat and black hat thinking to strengthen the idea. Finally, we assess the idea and compare it to alternative ideas. The generative green hat stage is the possibility, stage the stage of suggestions and proposals.

Green Hat Questioning

- What alternatives are we considering here?
- What other possible explanations could there be?
- Could we plan this in a new way?
- What ideas do we have to overcome these challenges?

Skills Developed

Skills include creative thinking and problem solving, vision and imagination, communication and confidence, a positive mental attitude and planning skills.

Key Learning Points

- Occassionaly invite learns to draw their ideas - this is a valuable alternative to language.
- If practised routinely, green hat thinking creates an environment of possibility and alternatives. It is used for designing a way forward.
- Green hat thinking works well after the black hat, coming up with ways to address the issues raised.
- Ideas are encouraged, and there is a move beyond the usual and expected.
- It is exciting, pioneering and provocative, removing us from our normal pattern of thinking.
- Green hat thinking requires exploration and curiosity.
- Sometimes, an idea is a provocation that helps move the thinking forward like stepping stones across a river.
- With green hat thinking, movement of perceptions and ideas occurs..

2. Learning the Hats — The Green Hat

▬ Example Green Hat Scenarios (Additional topics in section 4)

YOUNGER LEARNERS | **OLDER LEARNERS**

LEAD-IN (5 minutes)

Tree Wisdom

Learners are undertaking a project focused on trees. They have been to visit the local tree that takes pride of place in their school's forest area. They will get to climb it very soon. So that they really 'get to know' this tree, they have taken a photograph while out on a sensory walk and then looked at the detail of the tree's texture and discussed the risks associated with climbing it.

You now ask them to imagine the tree on the inside. What might be hidden? Generate as many ideas as possible with the children.

All creative responses are valid and not assessed, as they represent potential. The learners can draw their ideas and elaborate on them during an independent or teacher-directed session outside of the direct thinking hat session, where the thinking could be applied.

Potential Responses
- I think birds get together there each night and chat about their day. They share their food if some of them have had a bad day and haven't collected enough berries.
- I think that tree has space for a family – you know, those people who lived long ago and got preserved. That's where they go each night to feel safe.
- There's treasure. We have a history of pirates, around here. That tree looks harmless, but it protects the stolen treasure for the families of the pirates and only they know it's there.

Money, Money, Money

Finances are always under review in any home, business or organisation. As part of their financial awareness module, explain to the group that they are going to think of three areas around school where costs could be reduced – no response is too inventive.

Potential Responses
- Reduce the days that learners come to school and set home learning opportunities. Lighting and heating costs would be saved.
- Sell off excess land to local people or businesses. Rent out the spare spaces onsite as either a temporary or permanent solution.
- No paper or printing allowed, and ensure the technology is current, perhaps encouraging learners to use their own devices.
- Ask parents to donate on a termly basis to support the school budget.

Alternative lead-ins

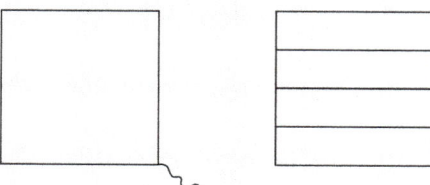

Begin by making a simple outline drawing of a square with a wiggly line trailing from one of the bottom corners. Then, ask the class for suggestions as to what the drawing might represent (a kite, a mouse trapped under a box, an overhead view of a leaking tank, etc.).

Then, make another simple drawing and ask what it could be. As learners make suggestions, point out that their suggestions are possibilities, creative ideas or alternatives. These are the sort of words you want to use to lead into the green hat concept.

Ask learners to make a diagram showing how the human head could be improved. Usually, this produces eyes on the back of the head, octopus-like tentacles, rearrangement of the hair, bigger ears, etc. Accept all ideas without comment since the green hat does not evaluate. Invite learners to trade diagrams or display their ideas so that all can see the variety of possibilities that the class has proposed.

2. Learning the Hats — The Green Hat

| Younger Learners | Older Learners |

EXPLANATION AND DEMONSTRATION (10 minutes)

A Room of My Own

Learners are asked to design their perfect bedroom so that it reflects their most creative thinking. Explain that they are to include three ideas that have never been thought about before.

Potential Responses
– A drawing of their design
– I would love fish in my room and lots of plants.
– I would remove my bed and sleep on the floor.
– I would want my bedroom to feel like my kingdom. I can see a crown painted on the wall, a throne and a dragon in the corner that is there just to protect me.
– My bedroom would be silent – not a sound – and it would be full of stars.

Community by Design

The local council is encouraging innovation in schools and would like entrants to design a town of the future that aims to include everyone. Your learners are keen to enter and are using this as part of their design portfolio. Thinking in new ways and following on from previous red and black hat thinking, you ask them to put on their green hats and think of at least five innovative themes to consider for the town.

Potential Responses
– A town with no cars or other vehicles.
– One tree in the town for each person living there.
– Reducing the need for transport and encouraging pedestrianisation, with centres that only allow bikes and scooters for all ages.
– Creating equitable living spaces that everyone can afford and investing in communal open spaces that encourage biodiversity and collective responsibility and are sustainable.

PRACTICE (15 minutes)

Bumper Crops

Your apple trees produce very desirable fruit, but unfortunately, many of the apples are wasted because they fall from the tree and are too damaged to use. What ideas do you have to prevent this from happening?

Potential Responses
– Make sure that every tree had a net underneath it so that when the apples fall, they don't hit the ground.
– You could use a sensor that sets off an alarm in your house as soon as one apple drops, and this would prompt you to go out and pick the rest.
– You could employ people on shifts so that there is always somebody there retrieving the apples.

A Little Help from Our Friends

You have been asked to design a computerised device to address one thing in your life that is a challenge for either yourself or somebody that you care about. You must devise a potential idea that may overcome the problem given thought and focus.

Potential Responses
– I want to think about something that would remind my mom to put her glasses, her phone and her keys in the same place every time she arrived home.
– My dad struggles to open jars and lift saucepans. I would love a device that would help him do those things that cause him pain.
– I'm thinking about a robot that can do some of my hockey practice for me; when it returns to the house, I can plug it in and accept the improvements if I want to.

deBono THE SIX THINKING HATS FOR SCHOOLS AND FAMILIES

2. Learning the Hats The Green Hat

Younger Learners & Older Learners

ELABORATION
(5 minutes)

Encourage reflective practice to answer the following questions:
- What did they notice?
- What went well?
- What challenges did they face when using the thinking skills?
- How could they improve their green hat thinking?
- Where will they use this type of thinking in their life?

Teacher modelling is useful too.

CONCLUSION
(5 minutes)

- Summarise the main points of the session.
- Describe how green hat thinking supports creative thinking where a search for alternatives is fundamental. There is a need to seek ideas beyond the normal pattern of thinking, and adding a provocation allows for this.
- Reflect on the thinking skill explored and developed in the session.

GREEN HAT DIALOGUE

'What if…'
'Imagine that…'
'We could do this, or this, or this.'
'Green hats now. This type of thinking makes my brain fizz.'
'Have you ever thought…?'
'I know this sounds crazy, but hear me out.'
'Green hats on – it's time for change.'
'I am good at green hat thinking; I can always think of lots of new ideas. '
'I write my ideas down; you never know, one day they might be worth a fortune.'
'Do you think Bill Gates is a great green hat thinker?', Yes, but I think he owns all the other hats as well.'
'I don't find story writing easy. Can I sit with my green hat on for a while, please?'
'You can use green hat in maths as well, you know. I am trying to take the simplest route here.'

Next Hat: Blue Hat

'The blue hat is like the conductor of the orchestra. The conductor gets the best out of the orchestra by seeing that what should be done is done at the right time.'

Dr Edward de Bono
'Six Thinking Hats.'

2.6
Blue Hat Summary

The blue hat is for organising the thinking, deciding what to think about and which hats to use, and drawing conclusions at the end.

'If you wait for opportunities to occur, you will be one of the crowd.'
Dr Edward de Bono

Your Notes

Tip: Before you teach the blue hat, we recommended that you read this section on the blue hat and sections 3.1 and 3.2 on systematic use and sequences together.

▬ Description of the Blue Hat

The blue hat is different from all of the other hats. The other hats are concerned with thinking about a particular situation. The blue hat is for thinking about the thinking that is being used – the process, not the content. This is 'meta-cognition'.

The blue hat is like the conductor of the orchestra, deciding what to think about and which hats to use and when. We can associate the blue hat with the blue sky. If we were up in the sky, we could look down and see what was happening on the ground below. With the blue hat, we rise above the thinking that is taking place to remain objective and to facilitate the process.

The blue hat is used to comment on and facilitate the thinking process. This can be short and simple by requesting that a specific hat be put on or taken off or that a switch in thinking from one hat to another occur. This might happen as a short intervention in a broader discussion using one or two hats. It is also possible to design and use a sequence of many hats to create a thinking agenda (see sections 3.1 and 3.2). The use of the blue hat varies depending on where we are in the thinking process.

When we begin to think about a situation, the blue hat is used to define the focus and decide which hat(s) to use to address the task. If we are going somewhere, it is useful to know where we are trying to go.

'Putting on our blue hats, let's decide what we want to think about and which hats we'll need to use.'

During the thinking, it might be necessary to use the blue hat to restate objectives, redefine the problem, provide a summary of the thinking so far, or decide the next step. The group's thinking may stray from the original purpose of the discussion.

'This is interesting, but I think we are drifting away from our goal. Who can wear the blue hat and recall our purpose?'

Restating means simply repeating the original thinking task to keep the thinkers on track: 'May I put on my blue hat to remind you that we are trying to think of all the creatures that might live in or near a pond?'

Alternatively, the discussion's purpose may change as the thinking unfolds. At such times, someone can put on the blue hat to redefine what the group is trying to do. Redefining indicates a change in the task: 'Putting on my blue hat, I would like to note that we have decided to stop thinking about where to have the class picnic until Julie checks on our transportation. Right now, we are going to think instead about what food we would like to serve'.

The blue hat is also used to conclude the thinking with a summary and outcome. This outcome can take the form of a solution, conclusion, choice or decision, design, plan or something else definite, such as a promise. There is always an outcome of some sort, even if it is not what we intended. The summary can describe what has and has not been achieved. For example, it can identify unresolved problems, obstacles and information gaps.

'I want to put on my blue hat here and ask if we can conclude.'

We are using the blue hat whenever we suggest the next hat to be used. The blue hat need not be explicitly acknowledged at every turn.

2. Learning the Hats — The Blue Hat

Purpose of Blue Hat Thinking

The blue hat signals detachment and overview and provides a structured approach for purposeful exploration. This is different from a free-flowing approach to discussion in which different modes of thinking are mixed. Blue hat thinking uses either a predetermined plan or spur-of-the-moment decisions to structure the conversation as necessary.

Blue Hat Questioning

- What is the purpose of our agenda? Have we been specific in defining the problem?
- Which hat are we using now? Do we need our black hat thinking on that one now that we understand the positives explored through our yellow hat?
- Can we summarise what we've discussed?
- What actions are needed? Who will undertake them and when?
- Do we need to reconvene once the missing information has been acquired?

Making Observations and Comments

Once thinking has begun, we may put on the blue hat to step back from the thinking to comment upon the thinking of another person, the group or ourselves.

— 'Putting on my blue hat, I feel that we have just been discussing what is wrong with this idea, and we should now think about how to improve it.'
— 'My blue hat thinking is that we are trying to think about two different things at once. Let's take them one at a time.'
— 'I'm putting on my blue hat to say that we have just had a great deal of red hat thinking.'
— 'I would like to put on my blue hat and see what we have done so far. It seems to me that we have made three decisions.'

The purpose of a blue hat comment is to be constructive. If we know what we are doing wrong, then we can try to put it right. It may be that the thinking has concentrated on only one part of a problem or that the group has become bogged down in an argument. The blue hat provides a mirror in which the thinkers can see their own thinking.

Time Keeping

Set a time limit for the thinking when using a hat. This ensures a brisk pace and prevents the thinking from going off track. The red hat can be used for less than one minute, while the other hats only need a few minutes each. You can always extend the time by a further few minutes if needed.

Skills Developed

Skills include communication, organisation and planning, responsiveness, situation assessment, collaboration, self-regulation, meta-cognition, people management, facilitation, team building, interpersonal skills and time management.

Key Learning Points

- The blue hat can be used to stage a brief intervention using one or two other hats. Alternatively, it can be used to design a sequence of many hats to address a particular situation.
- The blue hat can be used at the beginning, middle and end of a thinking sequence. It can be used to plan a way forward, ensure the thinking is addressing the key issue, summarise the thinking and draw

2. Learning the Hats — The Blue Hat

conclusions. Thinking is only useful if worthwhile actions follow.
- This hat is often worn by the person organising the discussion or meeting, but there is opportunity for any member of the group to suggest a need for specific modes of thinking at any time. This works if the blue hat is not overused and does not interrupt the flow of the thinking.
- The blue hat is neutral, objective and open – its purpose is to ensure good thinking, not a predetermined outcome.

Example Blue Hat Scenarios (Additional topics in section 4)

	YOUNGER LEARNERS	OLDER LEARNERS
LEAD-IN (5 minutes)	**Draw This** Ask the learners to pair up and sit back to back, with each learner assuming the role of either artist or instructor. Using an image that you have provided to the instructor, the artist will attempt to replicate it without seeing it through clear instruction from the instructor. How well do the drawings match? This will provide an opportunity for discussion around clarity, road mapping, and how knowing and communicating the steps of a process will lead to a more positive outcome. *Potential Responses* – The instructions weren't clear. I didn't know what I was supposed to be doing or thinking about. – I started to panic before we even started about getting it exactly right. I hate not knowing what something should look like at the end. – I didn't see the purpose of the activity. Why exactly did we need to draw a house?	**Missing Instructions** The teacher asks for two volunteers to put up a small tent at the front of the classroom. When the learners ask for the instructions, the teacher explains that the manufacturers failed to provide them. The audience's role is to notice behaviours, conversation and actions as the pair undertake their task. *Potential Responses* – They looked nervous once they knew there were no instructions to follow. – They were disorganised. The poles were everywhere, and they didn't seem to know how to sort them. They were in a bit of a panic but just continued anyway. – It took them a long while to talk to each other to think how they might begin, so they wasted time. – I felt sorry for them; they looked a bit lost. They would have preferred having a plan.
EXPLANATION AND DEMONSTRATION (10 minutes)	**Thank You** There is going to be an end-of-year party to thank all volunteers for supporting the school during the past year. The headteacher is collaborating with staff to organise this and has requested a learner representative from each class to help organise the collection of ideas. What skills must this person have to be successful? You are looking for the learners' developing understanding of a blue hat thinker.	**Every Day a Good Day** This could be useful as part of a study skills programme. The purpose of this activity is to become good at selecting which hat to use. As the teacher, model your approach to planning your week. What modes of thinking do you use? Talk through your choices as you plan so that the learners see and hear the blue hat thinking and witness the process. Make your use of the blue hat explicit.

52 | THE SIX THINKING HATS FOR SCHOOLS AND FAMILIES® • deBono

2. Learning the Hats — The Blue Hat

EXPLANATION AND DEMONSTRATION *(10 minutes)*

Younger Learners

Potential Responses
- They need to be good at encouraging other people to share their ideas.
- They need to be clear about what sort of ideas we need and what the result needs to be.
- They need to be aware, listen carefully and keep people focused on where ideas are needed.
- They need to be organised and punctual.
- They need to keep notes and do the things asked of them, checking that other people understand their jobs too.
- They need to be good at summarising and concluding.

Older Learners

Using the blue hat, ask learners to discuss which hats they would use to plan their week. It is not important at this stage to put the hats in a specific order. In groups, give learners two minutes each to share their reasoning and then invite a summary from each group.

Potential Responses
- I would use the red hat to see how I felt about the week ahead – what was I looking forward to and what was I dreading.
- I would use the white hat to list all the things I need to do and when I need to do them by.
- I would use the green hat to consider all possible things I could do.
- Maybe I would use the red hat to decide which activities were the priority.
- I would use the yellow hat to assess what would be the most valuable things to do during the week
- I would use the black hat to think about what the issues were in the week ahead, what problems might happen with my plan and what might happen if I don't do certain things.
- I would use the blue hat to summarise my plan.

Additional exercises

Ask learners to give some examples of blue hat statements that someone might use when thinking about thinking.

Potential Responses
- Wearing the blue hat is like being in the sky above, looking down at a situation and planning for the best way to think about it.
- The blue hat directs the thinking that is being done. It is for thinking about thinking. What kind of thinking should I do next?
- When the Six Thinking Hats are used, we can put on the blue hat to decide what other colour hats are needed.

deBono   THE SIX THINKING HATS FOR SCHOOLS AND FAMILIES® | 53

2. Learning the Hats — The Blue Hat

Younger Learners & Older Learners

EXPLANATION AND DEMONSTRATION (10 minutes)

Tell the learners to put on their blue hats and decide which thinking hats might be used to solve the following problems. They don't need to actually use the hats at this time.

– You are trying to decide what to wear to a costume party.

Potential Responses
🟢 I will come up with ideas.
🔴 I will make a choice or 🟡 then ⬛ I will evaluate my options.

– Someone you don't like insults you.

Potential Responses
🔴 I will try to understand how I feel.
⬜ I will gather the facts of what happened.
🟢 Are there other interpretations of what happened? What are my options for next steps?
🟡 then ⬛ I will evaluate my options.

– Your friend is accused of cheating on a test, but you know that he or she didn't.

Potential Responses
⬜ I will get the facts and ask my friend some questions.
🟢 I will explore options for action.

– You have been having a long argument with your mother, who wants you to clean up your room.

Potential Responses
🔴 Tell her how I feel.
⬜ Ask my mother how she feels.
🟡 It is unclear what the thought is here. Please clarify. Should this say something like 'Tidy up my room'?
🟢 Explore alternative ways of keeping my room tidy without it being annoying.

– A neighbour has a fierce guard dog that gets out through a hole in the fence. This dog has not yet bitten anyone, but it terrifies people. Use your blue hat to tell what hats you would use to think about this situation. Then go ahead and do the thinking. Finally, summarise your thinking and tell what you would do about the dog.

Potential Responses
🟦 Blue hat to plan at the beginning and
🟦 Blue hat to summarise at the end,
🟢 Green hat to create ideas on what to do
⬜ White hat to ask different people what they feel and think about the situation.

– Your parents tell you that you must spend Saturday mornings working around the house. You really don't like the idea, but you want to think about it. Use your blue hat to explain which three hats you will use to ponder the situation.

Potential Responses
🟡 What are the benefits?
⬜ What questions am I going to ask?
🟢 What alternative ideas could I propose to my parents?

54 | THE SIX THINKING HATS FOR SCHOOLS AND FAMILIES® ·!· deBono

2. Learning the Hats — The Blue Hat

Younger Learners | **Older Learners**

—The circus was planning to give three performances in town, but a sudden storm has wrecked the circus tent. Imagine that you are the owner of the circus. Put on your blue hat and describe the thinking that should now take place.

Potential Responses
- What are the benefits of the situation?
- What are my options?
- Which option am I going to take?

PRACTICE (15 minutes)

Story Time

The children in your class have agreed to become reading partners to a younger child in school. So that they are prepared for this responsibility, ask the groups to choose one of the Six Thinking Hats to think about this topic and explain why they chose it.

Potential Responses
- We wanted to share how we felt about...
- We decided to look for the positives, to motivate each other and to think about the benefits for us and the younger children.
- We needed to think about what we needed to think about. What did we need to consider and do to make this a successful activity?
- We need to think about the problems we might face.
- Do we need to know something about our partner? Do they need to know something about us?

Making Up for Lost Time

You have missed a considerable proportion of school and have asked your friends to help you think through a plan that will help you focus your time now that you are back on a part-time basis. Using their experience, you have asked them to plan a three-hat thinking sequence that you can use to create an effective timetable to follow.

Potential Responses
- What should my objective be for this timetable?
- What has been missed? What is important?
- Here are some ideas on the best way to catch up.

ELABORATION (5 minutes)

Encourage reflective practice to answer the following questions:
- What did they notice?
- What went well?
- What challenges did they face when using the thinking skills?
- How could they improve their blue hat thinking?
- Where will they use this type of thinking in their life?

CONCLUSION (5 minutes)

- Summarise the main points of the session.
- Describe how effective blue hat thinking is directive and responsive, observing the direction of the discussion and steering the thinking as needed to achieve the outcome. Blue hat intervention can also be used to restate or redefine the focus if the thinking has wandered off course.
- Reflect on the thinking skill explored and developed in the session.

BLUE HAT DIALOGUE

'If we are going to have any chance of winning this netball tournament, we need a plan, Chloe.'
'So, where do we begin? My thinking is that feelings are high here, so shall we begin with red hat exploration?'
'That was a great discussion, but what are we going to do about it? We need actions.'

2. Learning the Hats — The Blue Hat

Younger Learners & Older Learners

BLUE HAT DIALOGUE

'I know you are nervous about the sleepover, Molly. Would it help if you knew what was planned?'

'It doesn't really matter what we talk about – let's just get better at thinking.'

'I like to know what's going on, and I am quite bossy. If I like suggesting where we go next, does that make me a blue hat thinker?'

'It is really useful to stop halfway through and summarise the discussion. This helps me see what is important and what we need to do next.'

'What have we just decided? I am not sure we have got all the facts, can we go over that Summary again, please?'

---

*'If you understand the system,
you can design appropriate action.'*

Dr Edward de Bono
'Think! Before It's Too Late'

3 *How to Use the Hats*

3.1.
The Systematic Use of the Thinking Hats

What Have We Learned?

Throughout the previous chapters, you revisited the pedagogy that creates an effective working environment and consolidated your understanding of the learner's right to think and be respected for it. Familiarity with different modes of thinking, and the associated language, and purposeful use of questions creates the opportunity to develop specific skills that can be taught and developed using each hat.

Both you and your learners should now be familiar with each of the hats and have engaged in sufficient practice to apply this thinking effectively across a range of scenarios, putting the relevant hat on and taking it off as required. You should know how to use these models to have fun teaching while your learners are being motivated to think.

You will have used individual hats in isolation to access a particular idea using a specific mode of thinking or to engage in a conversation or learning discussion. Through routine and focused teaching, it does not take long for the hats to become an integrated language for signalling a thinking direction and redirecting that thinking if it fails to achieve the desired outcome.

Reviewing Single Use of the Hats

You could use this three-part mini review session to evaluate both your own and the learners' developing understanding of and sophistication regarding using the hats. You could even design your own review approach. It might be an interesting exercise to consider the preferential modes of from both your own perspective and that of the learners, questioning the dominant form of thinking and the impact this has on the discussion.

Remember that the purpose of the Six Thinking Hats is to develop the capacity to use all six modes of thinking and to prevent the dominance of a few preferred modes. This will lead to greater effectiveness.

1. **Identify as many thoughts about butterflies as you can using each hat. You can add to the examples below.**
   - ⚪ A butterfly gets essential nutrients from drinking from mud puddles. Many butterfly colonies are in danger of extinction.
   - 🔴 I worry that some butterflies are in danger of extinction.
   - ⚫ Temperature variability is putting the butterfly population at risk. This is because butterflies need an ideal body temperature of about 85 degrees Fahrenheit to fly.
   - 🟡 Butterflies pollinate the plants in your garden, which makes it possible for more plants to grow.
   - 🟢 We need ideas to protect butterflies from climate change.
   - 🔵 How might we develop our thinking further?

2. **Which hats are being worn in these statements?**
   —We have 32% girls in this classroom. ⚪
   —That is not fair. I am outraged. 🔴
   —If we got lost, how well prepared would we be? ⚫
   —I feel sick at the very thought of that suggestion. 🔴

3. How to Use the Hats

—My mom told me that there was snow on the way. .... 🎩 (white)
—Let's think of another way to solve that. .... 🎩 asking for 🟢 (blue asking for green)
—I can see how the online library would work for so many people, as it is easy to access. .... 🟡 (yellow)

3. Which hats would you switch to in the following situations?
—There is an increasingly negative approach to the discussion. .... 🟡 (yellow)
—There is confusion as to what needs to be achieved and why. .... 🔵 (blue)
—There has been a shift to a very sensitive subject. .... 🔴 (red)
—When asked for their comments, everyone continues to be super positive. .... ⚫ (black)
—The same people are suggesting ideas. .... 🔵 asking for 🟢
    from those who are quiet
—A new theme for learning is being planned. .... 🟢 (green)
—There are too many gaps in the information required to move forward. .... ⬜ (white)
—Before moving on, we need a plan. .... 🔵 (blue)

Using a Sequence of Hats

In addition to putting on single hats, we can use sequences of more than one hat to give structure and direction to the thinking. This is a useful tool when there are different strongly held viewpoints or when the discussion has lost focus. Sequences provide steps for carrying out more complex thinking operations. Learning, discussing and negotiating sample sequences is an excellent way to reinforce the role of each hat.

The sequence of hats depends on what the objective is. Sequences can be used by individuals organising their own thinking or by groups of people. If you are working in a group, then it is helpful to have a designated facilitator. whose role is to ensure the disciplined use of the hats. The facilitator controls a change of hats. Keep the time allotted to each hat to a few minutes only so that the thinking is focused and momentum is maintained. You may always add a few more minutes if needed. It is much better to set a short time and extend than have unlimited time and risk losing momentum and focus.

The blue hat should always be used at the beginning and end of a sequence to plan and conclude the thinking.

The initial blue hat establishes the following:
🔵 Why we are here and what we want to achieve.
🔵 What we are thinking about – the possible definitions of the problem or situation.
🔵 The background to the thinking and a plan for the sequence of hats to be used.

The final blue hat summarises the following:
🔵 What we have achieved – the outcome, conclusion, design, solution, and next steps.

Key Learning Points

- Most thinking sessions will start and end with the blue, which may also be needed to steer the process mid-session. At the beginning, the blue hat determines the focus of the discussion and the sequence of hats to be used; mid-flow, the blue hat summarises the progress and redirects the focus as needed. At the end, the blue hat summarises the thinking and plans the next steps.
- Choose only the hats you need; you don't have to use all six.
- There is no single best hat sequence. The sequence will vary with the theme and with the learner's thinking. Each hat can be used any number of times. For instance, in an idea-generating session, you may want to use the green hat several times. Where there are strong feelings at the outset, you might

want to use the red hat at the beginning, middle and end to see whether the discussion is altering the emotional temperature.
- As the facilitator, the teacher should discuss the sequence with the group and continue to wear the blue hat to manage the thinking and overall process. Once knowledge, skill and confidence have been achieved, certain learners may be trained to become facilitators.
- Plan your sequences, allowing a few minutes per hat. It is suggested that you allow 30 seconds maximum for the red hat. Extend the time in short spates if either the discussion or the needs of the specific cohort require it.

Types of Sequencing

Fixed Sequences
Where time permits, develop a sequence of hats in advance (a fixed sequence). Choosing a fixed sequence supports the need for a clear, uncomplicated discussion focus and definite results from the session.

Example

Contingent and flexible sequences
There may be times when the discussion takes an unexpected turn and you need to rely on a more responsive sequence that serves needs of the group and the desired outcome.

In this situation, the fixed sequence has some points at which you may make a reasoned choice about the next hat to use based on the conversation. For example, you may have started a discussion with red hat thinking. Should the red hat thinking show strong opposition to the idea, then it will make sense to follow with the black hat to see how much logical basis there is for the opposition. But if the red hat shows strong support, then you will want to follow with the yellow hat for the same reasons.

Example

Evolving sequences
These are used as part of more extended thinking sessions where there is a complicated matter to explore. The longer a sequence, the less responsive it is to how the thinking develops. An evolving sequence or a series of shorter sequences allows for more flexibility.

Remember: Do not allow flexibility to become so casual that disciplined thinking is lost and the discussion becomes unstructured and unfocused.

3. How to Use the Hats

Examples of Thinking Sequences

First Ideas

In the initial stages of generative thinking, the focus is made clear under the blue hat, followed by the collection of information already held or required under the white hat and an opportunity to generate further possibilities freely using the green hat.

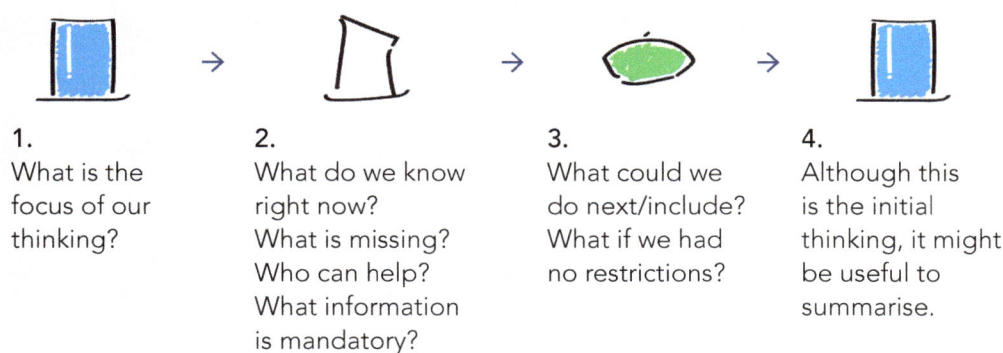

1.
What is the focus of our thinking?

2.
What do we know right now?
What is missing?
Who can help?
What information is mandatory?

3.
What could we do next/include?
What if we had no restrictions?

4.
Although this is the initial thinking, it might be useful to summarise.

Practice example: A change of plan
There is a proposal for a new approach to parents' evenings. Parents will be asked to use a Six Thinking Hats sequence to discuss the learners progress, motivation and how they can support further development. Use the First Ideas sequence to evaluate and improve on this proposal.

Emotions

This is a sequence that is used when there are strong feelings about a situation. First, we recognise the feelings held before exploring the facts with white hat objectivity. The green hat releases our creativity to create possible action, and the blue hat supports the thinking structure from discussion to action.

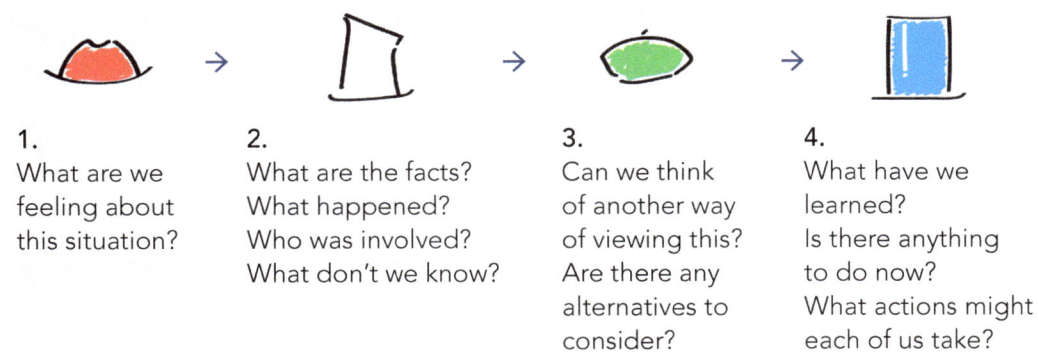

1.
What are we feeling about this situation?

2.
What are the facts?
What happened?
Who was involved?
What don't we know?

3.
Can we think of another way of viewing this?
Are there any alternatives to consider?

4.
What have we learned?
Is there anything to do now?
What actions might each of us take?

Practice example: To be, or not to be
The relationship between two close friends has become untenable. It is having a negative impact on them, the people they socialise with, their learning relationships and the quality of their work in sessions. As a trained school mediator, you are asked to navigate the discussion using the thinking hat sequence above.

3. How to Use the Hats

Quick Assessment

This sequence will help you identify whether an idea is worth pursuing. If there are no benefits you may as well stop the discussion; if there are benefits, then the blue hat summarises the positive aspects.

 →

1.
What are the good points?

2.
Let's summarise the benefits.
What happens next?

Practice example: What's not to like?
The school has decided to reduce onsite learning to four days a week. Learners are asked to discuss this.

Evaluation

Here, the value of the idea or suggestion is the focus. It is always advised to focus on the yellow hat before the black hat: if there are limited benefits, then there is no need to spend time looking at the issues.

1.
What benefits do we see that will add value to our idea? What is great about the suggestion we have made?

2.
What are the potential risks here? What do we need to be mindful of?

Practice example: Let's get moving!
A qualified secondary school teacher who originally trained as a play leader is bringing new ideas to the sessions. She has decided that one day a week, she will remove all furniture from the classroom. The learners are asked to trial this with a view to having an evaluation on this change at the end of the month.

Direct Action

This sequence is a precautionary one and ensures that decisions are considered in an empathic but risk-alert manner.

1.
What do we want to do, and what feelings is that generating?

2.
What could go wrong?
What situations might need considering?

Practice example: Moving in
As part of a diverse project on community, the pupils are asked to consider a range of sites that are being suggested for a local village to relocate to. The three sites suggested are the middle of a woodland, the foot of a mountain and the bank of a huge river.

Improvement

The black hat's cautious yet constructive role is essential for any chance of possible or necessary improvement to take place. The green hat is then used for a generative response, creating opportunities and solutions.

 →

1.
What are the weaknesses of this suggestion?

2.
What ideas can we generate that would overcome them?

Practice example: Culinary secrets
Three learners have received negative feedback from their cookery teacher. She has identified that the quality of their effort is not in doubt but that their end product is consistently below the required standard. They have been sent to discuss the challenges they face with each other before coming up with three ideas to improve before the teacher offers her own input.

Explanation

A situation has occurred that requires explanation. The white hat gives the facts about the situation, and the green hat presents positive reasons as to why it may have happened. There may be a consensus that one of the generated possibilities is the most likely.

 →

1.
What exactly do we know about the situation?

2.
Can we explore the possible explanations?

Practice example: It's a wrap!
How do you gift wrap an elephant?

Generating Possibilities

The green hat is the birthplace of possibility. The blue hat has a role in managing the green hat thinking, collecting and categorising the ideas generated.

 →

1.
What are the possibilities?
What if…?

2.
Can we summarise and organise our ideas and possibilities?

3. How to Use the Hats

Practice example: If only…
A small group of pupils are having trouble learning mathematical concepts in the classroom. You decide to ask them to think of ways that they could develop their maths and problem-solving skills in other ways. They may take time to 'warm up'. As all teachers know, if self-efficacy is low, pupils may demonstrate behaviours that do not support their efforts. So, start from a point of strength identification.

Caution

Here is an opportunity to focus specifically on potential danger and any need for caution. This sequence is purely about avoiding catastrophe.

1.
What do we know about the situation?
What do the statistics tell us?
Is this verified information?

2.
What are the risks?
Where are the dangers?

Practice example: Flying high
Bungee jumping is a 'the best of days, the worst of days' kind of situation, but the kudos lasts forever if you are successful. You and your siblings and granddad are planning to do your very first jump. Your granddad is insisting on approaching it with caution.

Opportunity

Here, we check the value of an idea or proposal. We consider first the facts and then the positives. This is the opposite of cautious thinking.

1.
What facts do we already know about the situation?

2.
What are the benefits?

Practice example: In business
An opportunity to set up 'teenage business ventures' is advertised across your region. You are expected to follow what your family believe to be the traditional route into university, but you have other ideas. You love baking and already make a significant profit at weekends supplying your local bakery with bread and cakes. You want to convince your parents that the idea to work vocationally is the best route for you.

Design

This sequence is useful to provide a structure for a creative design brief. The blue hat provides the brief's structure and purpose. The creative thinking under the green hat creates a range of possible ideas, and the red hat thinking provides an opportunity for the designer/s to use their intuition and express whether they feel a design would work or not. A logical assessment can be carried out later.

3. How to Use the Hats

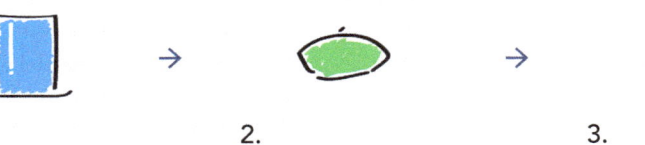

1. What is the design brief?
2. What are the possible designs?
3. How do we feel about each design?

Practice example: A learning space
As part of a design and technology programme, you are invited to design a classroom that makes learning about maths an experience that you can see and hear.

Usable Alternatives

The yellow hat takes a possibility one stage further, strengthening it to an alternative choice.

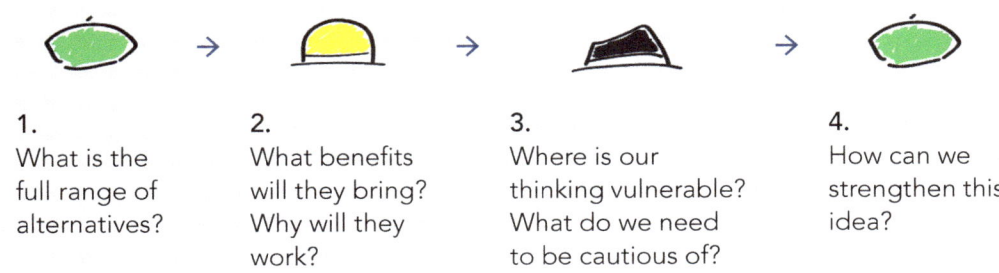

1. What is the full range of alternatives?
2. What benefits will they bring? Why will they work?
3. Where is our thinking vulnerable? What do we need to be cautious of?
4. How can we strengthen this idea?

Practice example: Moving towards...
From the Design scenario above, develop two ideas further into usable alternatives using this sequence.

Making a Choice

Modern life provides many of us with an abundance of choices that can be overwhelming. The ability to make the most appropriate choice in a situation is a valuable skill. The yellow and black hats help us evaluate the benefits and risks. Under the red hat, we make a decision based on our values and what matters most to us. If a decision is not reached, then learners can continue to generate further possibilities.

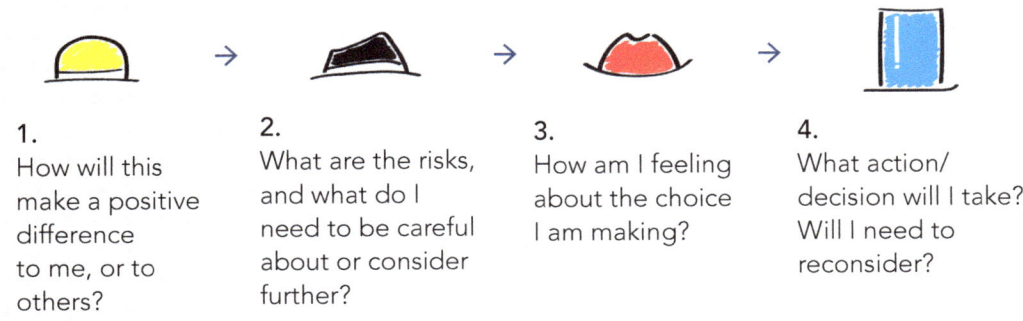

1. How will this make a positive difference to me, or to others?
2. What are the risks, and what do I need to be careful about or consider further?
3. How am I feeling about the choice I am making?
4. What action/decision will I take? Will I need to reconsider?

3. How to Use the Hats

Practice example: Party time
One of your learners will soon have their first birthday party at seven years old. The birthday boy would like help deciding on whether to hold a fancy dress party or not. There has been no decision despite weeks of conversation. The family have asked you to help, so you throw it to the children in your session using this sequence.

Remember: This is not an exhaustive list, and a sequence is only useful if it progresses the thinking.

With younger learners or those who find the sequences difficult, you might wish to introduce a shorter list: First Ideas, Evaluation, Improvement, Direct Action, Opportunity and Making a Choice.

'If we want young people to develop their habits of thinking for themselves, using their imagination, being open to new ideas, saying when they don't understand, and exploring real challenges together, then they have to see their teachers doing the same thing.'

Guy Claxton, cognitive scientist
specialising in the nature of real-world intelligence

Your Thinking Sequences

3.2 Six Thinking Hats Sequences

First Ideas

 →  →  →

1. What is the focus of our thinking?
2. What do we know right now? What is missing? Who can help? What information is mandatory?
3. What could we do next/include? What if we had no restrictions?
4. It might be useful to summarise the thinking.

Emotions

 → → →

1. What are you feeling about this situation?
2. What are the facts? What happened? Who was involved? What don't we know?
3. Can we think of another way of viewing this? Are there any alternatives to consider?
4. What have we learned? Is there anything to do now? What actions might each of us take?

Quick Assessment

 →

1. What are the good points?
2. Let's summarise the benefits. What happens next?

Evaluation

 →

1. What benefits do we see that will add value to our idea? What is great about the suggestion we have made?
2. What are the potential risks here? What do we need to be mindful of?

Direct Action

 →

1. What do we want to do, and what feelings is that generating?
2. What could go wrong? What situations might need considering?

Improvement

 →

1. What are the weaknesses of this suggestion?
2. What ideas can we generate that would overcome them?

Explanation

1. What exactly do we know about the situation?

→

2. Can we explore the possible explanations?

Generating Possibilities

1. What are the possibilities? What if…?

→

2. Can we summarise and organise our ideas and possibilities?

Caution

1. What do we know about the situation? What do the statistics tell us? Is this verified information?

→

2. What are the risks? Where are the dangers?

Opportunity

1. What facts do we already know about the situation?

→

2. What are the benefits?

Design

1. What is the design brief?

→

2. What are the possible designs?

→

3. How do we feel about each design?

Usable Alternatives

1. What is the full range of alternatives?

→

2. What benefits will they bring? Why will they work?

→

3. Where is our thinking vulnerable? What do we need to be cautious of?

→

4. How can we strengthen this idea?

Making a Choice

1. How will this make a positive difference to me, to others?

→

2. What are the risks, and what do I need to be careful about or consider further?

→

3. How am I feeling about the choice I am making?

→

4. What action/decision will I take? Will we need to reconsider?

3.3
Experiencing Sequential Thinking

> *'If you don't design your future, someone or something else will design it for you.'*
>
> Dr Edward de Bono

■ The Skills Developed

Consider the skills the Six Thinking Hats method encourages: using thinking and knowledge to design purposeful action; developing reasoning, logic and generative thinking; identifying the significance of emotional expression in the thinking process; having positive mental attitudes and caution; understanding the importance of growth and development, collaboration and the power of parallel thinking; being flexible; and being able to switch mental modes of thought to serve the thinking process.

■ Key Learning Points

- Parallel thinking is when everyone uses the same mode of thinking simultaneously. The energy is directed at using that thinking mode well, rather than winning an argument. This promotes exploration and development of ideas.
- The Six Thinking Hats approach separates out potentially conflicting modes of thinking, making the process more productive and enjoyable.
- The blue hat's role is to ensure an effective use of the hats. The content of thinking is the responsibility of everyone in the group.
- A sequence occurs when any two or more hats are used one after the other.
- Learners can explore their thinking with confidence, as there is no right or wrong sequence of hats, only more or less effective ones.
- When thinking is clear, structured and simple, it becomes more enjoyable and effective.
- Learners who engage with the Six Thinking Hats concept deal with one mode of thinking at a time, but they can also switch their thinking when the need arises.
- It is possible to turn effective thinking into a game, ensuring all learners develop good thinking habits in a safe, controlled and inspiring environment.
- Thinkers can engage in a formal structure, planned at the outset, or follow a line of discussion, putting on one hat or another as required. They can even nominate a change in hats to serve the exploration of thought.
- The more effectively learners understand and follow the rules of engagement, the more effective the thinking and outcome.

3. How to Use the Hats

Sequence Planning

| YOUNGER LEARNERS | OLDER LEARNERS |

LEAD-IN
(5 minutes)

Come Rain or Shine!

Request that learners focus their thinking on creating new designs for umbrellas. Ask them to be ready to contribute to the teacher-modelled planning session. Share your thoughts as you move through your sequence so that the pupils understand that the choice of hats is purposeful.

- 🔵 What were the reasons for choosing umbrellas as our topic?
- ⚪ What do we already know? (Clarify how accurately they understand the information they are offering.) Do you know of any experts that might be able to contribute information to the topic?
- 🟢 Is there something that you would really love to learn? Something new and exciting? Something others may not have thought of but would enjoy?
- 🔴 What are your initial feelings about the project? (Refer to environmental clues shared in previous chapters that might help them express their feelings.)

You may want to include the red hat here just to gauge levels of motivation.

The Power of Youth

You are about to begin a topic on the 'rights of children past and present'.

Explain that you want the learners to collaborate with you in planning the unit. What might they like to understand that they might not know now? What questions do they have?

Invite the learners to interact with their group and decide how they will use the thinking hats to plan their thinking process, advising them that it will take more than one hat to think about this. Then, call them back as a group and, wearing the blue hat, model the design process, inviting contribution.

- 🔵 What are you being asked to do? What will success look like?
- 🟡 What are the benefits of including you in the planning process?
- ⚪ What do you already know about the rights of children? Do you know of any famous campaigners you could research for more information? Where might you be able to access information that is lacking?
- 🟢 What type of activities would you like to engage in? How might your environment change to reflect your learning?
- ⚫ Are there any risks involved in any of the current suggestions? What might your need to be cautious of?
- 🔵 What have we discussed so far? What are our next steps? What actions are needed, and who needs to ensure that they happen?

Remember: Learners do not need to do detailed thinking under each hat; they are only creating a plan regarding which hats to use.

EXPLANATION AND DEMONSTRATION
(10 minutes)

Young and older learners but adapted for the level of sophistication

Just Chillin'

Conservationists monitor penguin colonies to assess the effect of climate change on their breeding success and survival. A range of data is vital to creating management plans to help preserve the conditions that the penguins need to thrive and to aiding governments in advocating for sustainable policy.

The penguins in the king penguin colony in St Andrew's Bay on South Georgia need to be counted and the area of the breeding colony evaluated.

→

Younger Learners & Older Learners

EXPLANATION AND DEMONSTRATION *(10 minutes)*

Ask learners to design a thinking sequence that will help produce a report to support the work of conservation action groups.

You can use the sequence below as a scaffold. With more confident sequence planners, ask them to design their own.

🟦 Blue hat
- What are we trying to achieve?
- What does a successful outcome look like?
- Who do we need to add to the thinking team?

🟨 Yellow hat
- Why is it a good idea to monitor populations?
- What is going/went well?
- Which skills/techniques are useful?

⬜ White hat
- What do we know about this topic already? What else do we need to know?
- What data do learners require for the census? What is missing?
- Where will we locate the information we need?
- What skills do we have already that can help us in this?

🔴 Red hat
- How do you feel about species loss/extinction and the role humans play in it?
- What are your feelings about this task?
- How did you feel while you were learning about the population?

⬛ Black hat
- What might make this task difficult?
- With the density and number of penguins (250,000 pairs in one colony plus chicks), how do you know you aren't recounting individuals?
- What else might make the counting inaccurate?
- What are we finding difficult?

🟢 Green hat
- How can we overcome the challenges we have considered? Is there technology that might serve us?

🟦 Blue hat
- What have we achieved?
- Are the numbers we are calculating feasible and reliable given what we know about previous populations?
- What further tasks might we need to undertake?
- Do we need to go back and rethink aspects of what we are doing?
- What information can we provide to the relevant conservation bodies?
- What action do you think would help sustain the penguin populations?

PRACTICE *(15 minutes)*

The following examples are for learners to engage with independently, either individually or in small groups. Emphasise the focus being on the thinking skills and not the content of the scenario. Assign a limit time for each exercise, keeping the potential of your learners in mind. Ask them to choose an example from the sequences provided in the previous chapter or to create one of their own if they have reasoned this out.

3. How to Use the Hats

	Younger Learners	Older Learners

PRACTICE *(15 minutes)*

Younger Learners

Pen Pal Poetry

As part of your 'hands across the sea, project, you have been asked to write to your pen pal and describe yourself in poetic form. Using your developing knowledge of the Six Thinking Hats, design a sequence that will help you structure your approach to this project.

Potential Response:
- White Hat
- Yellow Hat
- Black Hat
- Green Hat
- Blue Hat

Older Learners

Up, Up and Away

A hot air balloon ride over the Sahara Desert has gone terribly wrong, and the friends are bound for disaster. How should they approach this problem through a thinking sequence?

Potential Response:
- Green Hat
- Yellow Hat
- Black Hat
- Green Hat
- Blue Hat

ELABORATION *(5 minutes)*

Encourage reflective practice to answer the following questions:
- What did they notice?
- What went well?
- What challenges did they face when using the planned sequences? How did they adapt?
- Where will they use this type of thinking in their life?

Teacher modelling is useful too. It is crucial that learners witness adults applying, talking through and explaining their authentic use of the hats. Over time, fluent use of the hats will develop, with learners leading their own thinking and observing that of others.

CONCLUSION *(5 minutes)*

- Summarise the main points of the session.
- Invite learners to describe how they found the process of designing sequences. Was there more than one effective sequence?
- Reflect on the thinking skills explored and developed and the benefits they may have for broader aspects of their lives.
- As fluency increases and flow occurs, you may want to introduce a range of stretch and challenge opportunities into your sessions.

SELF- AND PEER ASSESSMENT OPPORTUNITY. Can also be used for teacher evaluation of the session *(5 minutes)*

- Did you follow the plan, and did it give you the results you wanted?
- How do you feel the session went?
- What went well during the session? What benefits did it offer?
- What needs strengthening?
- What facts support this evaluation? What could you add so that your session will work for all thinkers?
- What could you do differently next time?
- What actions will you take?

3. How to Use the Hats

Additional activity: Make flags (or bunting) for some or all of the sequences. Each coloured hat can become one vertical band. For example, the First Ideas flag would have a blue band on the left, a white band in the centre and a green band on the right.

'If you never change you mind, why have one.'

Dr Edward de Bono

4 Additional Practice Topics

4.1
All-weather Bike

All-weather bike

New! All-weather bike has a brightly coloured umbrella to protect the rider from rain, sleet, snow, wind and sun. No more wet hair or ruined clothes. Ride in comfort no matter what the forecast!

⌂ White Hat

What white hat questions do you have about this design?

Potential Responses
- Was this designed for a particular country or climate?
- Has this been tested, and if so, what were the results?
- Who is the bike designed for?

🎩 Red Hat

What red hat statements do you have about this design?

Potential Responses
- I would feel unsafe.
- I would feel silly.
- I like it.
- It's funny.

4. Additional Practice Topics

▲ Black Hat

What black hat observations do you have about this design?

Potential Responses
−The umbrella could snag on things.
−A gust of wind might catch the umbrella like a sail and throw the bicycle off balance.
−The front of the umbrella hangs over the front wheel instead of covering the rider, so that part is wasted.
−Rain, sleet, snow and wind might blow in from the side and hit the rider.
−The assembly of this bicycle might be difficult.

🟡 Yellow Hat

What yellow hat observations do you have about this design?

Potential Responses
−The umbrella would protect you from the sun, reducing the chance of sunburn and keeping you cooler.
−It would be difficult to go too fast with this bike, which might make it safer.
−Other people would easily see this bike, which might mean fewer collisions.
−If the wind is blowing from behind, it might push the bike along.

🟢 Green Hat

What green hat ideas do you have about improving this design?

Potential Responses
−The umbrella could be changed to a more aerodynamic design to reduce the wind resistance.
−The umbrella or weather covering could be detachable.
−Perhaps there could be a sort of windscreen in front of the rider.
−What about a helmet with an attachable cape that is clipped onto the bike?
−Invite learns to draw their new design.

🟦 Blue Hat

If you have been using this exercise to teach the other hats, then you can ask the learners to do a blue hat summary of their thinking.

If you have not yet used this exercise, then ask the learners to propose a sequence for evaluating and improving this design. They can then use the sequence.

Potential Responses

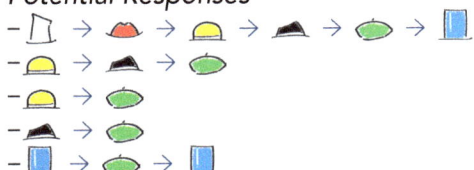

4.2 White Hat Practice

Younger Learners

Write On!
The headteacher has asked you to write the first school newsletter. What do you already know that will help? What information do you need? Where might you find that missing information?

Possible Responses
— We have been told that our audience will be parents, governors and teachers and may include members of the local community. Do we know what might interest them, and if not, how will we find out?
— My mom said that she would like to hear about any school visits and what the classes were during that week. My dad said he would like a 'My favourite lesson' section written by a teacher or pupil.
— We could look at other school newsletters and identify what we might use, adapt and improve.

Newsround
Watch a short news report. For example, here is a BBC *Newsround* report on how gravity works: https://www.youtube.com/watch?v=n40OmR6Rvpo
Identify as many facts as you can in two minutes. Share them with your talk partner at the end of the two minutes to check that what you have recorded are facts and to see what information you may have missed.

Possible Responses
— Scientists have been trying to understand how gravity works for hundreds of years.
— Sir Isaac Newton was a scientist who lived about 400 years ago and believed that an invisible force pulled things together. Einstein was a scientist who improved on Sir Isaac Newton's thinking.
— People use telescopes to understand how gravity works.
— What else do we want to find out or check?

Older Learners

My Team
Your head of year has asked you to create a presentation to persuade younger learners to enrol in your team sport for the following year. You can only use factually correct information as your guide. What key points will you cover?

Possible Responses
Dance
— It makes you happy and maintains interest when you move to music you love.
— Dance develops your sense of rhythm and co-ordination.
— It provides you with an opportunity to increase your aerobic fitness and muscular strength.

Running
— You can run throughout the week, either on your own, with your family and friends, or as part of a group.
— You can follow a programme, such as Couch to 5K, or just run freely.
— Running increases your lifespan and improves your ability to relax and sleep.

Football
— It keeps you active and disciplined.
— It teaches you how to be part of a team, focus your attention and follow a plan.
— It teaches the importance of practice and precision.

Born to Run

You are planning to run a marathon with a friend to raise money for a local charity. What do you need to know to make a success of the run and the fundraising?

Possible Responses
— That my training programme is efficient and will prepare me well. Are there any apps that I could use to support my effort?
— The time I want to achieve and what distances and times I have run to date.
— I know that my diet will need to be protein rich and that I need to increase my water intake. But I need more information to plan a healthy eating and drinking routine.

4.3
Red Hat Practice

Younger Learners

Am I Safe?
In a world that can often feel uncertain, encouraging a sense of safety for children is important. So that they can develop empathy for others with different experiences, it is important that they understand when they are safe. You can use images to explore the experiences of others in a range of situations and then use questions to elicit the learners' feelings.

— Where do you feel most safe?
— What does safe feel like in the body and mind?
— How strongly do they feel about something on a scale of 1-10, where 1 is low and 10 is high?
— What do you do to make somebody else feel welcome, comfortable and happy?

Potential Responses
— I feel calm in my bedroom when I am reading my books and my 'Do not disturb' sign is on the door.
— I am a little bit scared when it thunders; I don't like any loud noises. I am too embarrassed to tell people.
— I feel miserable when my dad suggests a swim in the sea. I stay grumpy all day!
— I am always excited to go to my nanna's house. When she teaches me how to use her sewing machine, I feel excited and peaceful at the same time.

What's Topical?
Identify an appropriate story that has caught the headlines. Share it with the learners and ask them to talk to a partner/in a small group about how the story made them feel. Remind them about how to 'red hat' correctly.

Potential Responses
— That story made me smile.
— I feel a little worried.
— I am excited.

Older Learners

Back to Basics
As part of an initiative to understand the impact of too much screen time on the mental wellness of young people, the school has asked parents to support it in a screen time amnesty. The school is suggesting that families refrain from using any digital device and instead engage in alternative activities.

— How do you think your parents might feel about this?
— What are you currently feeling?

4. Additional Practice Topics

Potential Responses
Parents
— That is such a promising idea.
— I am very doubtful that this will have any impact. Not sure how I feel right now.
— Absolutely not. I am irritated that the school feels that they can interfere with what happens at home.

Learners
— Have you read the research? We should all be backing this idea; I cannot wait to share my ideas.
— I am just thinking of the board games I might have to play. Bored already!
— I am grateful to the school for thinking that this is important.

Keep On Moving

The school has invited parents to a meeting to discuss an initiative it's about to trial. To maintain or improve pupils' physical health, staff are adding a compulsory physical activity to the lunchtime curriculum. All learners will sign up for at least one of these activities. The choices offered are running, dance, basketball or a gym session with a trained instructor. What red hat thinking might we expect?

Potential Responses
Parents
— It is a great idea, and I am thankful that the opportunity is there. But I am worried that making it compulsory is not a sensible way forward. I am concerned that there has been too little thought here.
— This is a terrific opportunity. I would be happy to support it.
— I am worried that this will make my son extremely anxious.

Learners
— I am thrilled.
— I really hate the thought. When in the day can we be left to just chat? Every day is a no-go for me.
— Either way, I am not bothered, but I am certainly not going to a club I am not interested in.

NB: *Remember that learners are not required to explain their feelings; developing the thinking further is the role of other hats.*

4.4
Black Hat Practice

Younger Learners

Riding the Waves
The pupils are planning a whitewater rafting adventure. To raise awareness of the risks involved, ask them to identify key black hat questions that they would like answered.

Potential Responses
—We need to check that everyone can swim.
—We have not done this before and might make a mistake.
—What happens if I fall in? I would like to know how somebody gets me back into the boat. How do I help others if they fall in?
—What mistakes have other children made? What can we learn from them?

Raising the Drawbridge
The learners are designing and building a castle that needs to keep the king, queen and courtiers safe. They have listened to a story and visited a castle as part of a school trip. They have sketched and taken photographs of castles, discussing their merits using a range of thinking skills. Now, they need to decide on how to apply this thinking as they plan their castle design. Encourage the pupils to question the potential success of their build.

Potential Responses
—I do not think making our castle out of wood is good enough. We need stronger, fire-resistant material like stone to stop people getting in or burning the castle down.
—We decided to put our castle on the top of a hill to make it more difficult for soldiers to get to. This will make carrying the stone up the hill hard work. We will need to recruit lots of local people – will this be expensive? How willing would they be to work for us?
—How will we stop the enemy from firing weapons up from the bottom of the hill?
—Which castles came under attack most throughout history? Did they all have a common weakness?

Older Learners

Working Together
The local community are raising money to improve the community centre.

Five proposals are being presented for funding. So that we can contribute to the discussions, please apply your black hat thinking to each situation.

—A weekly film club for the over-50s.
—A yoga class for moms and babies.
—A youth club for teenagers on a Friday evening.
—A learning hub for local school children to use over the weekends and holidays.
—Restoration of the skateboard area in the local park.

Potential Responses
—I think most over-50s are still working, aren't they? And those who aren't probably get together with friends anyway, and the take-up would be low. I am not sure this would be effective use of funding.
—Can you focus on yoga that is for moms and babies at the same time?
—Residents might not go for this. It could promote bad feeling.
—This would need staffing by teachers, and they already work long hours.

I'm Out of Here!
Each group must nominate a person take part in an 'I'm a Celebrity, Get Me Out of Here' experience. Using black hat thinking only, describe the challenges and problems you would face in a bid to put your case forwards.

Potential Responses
—I am shy, so it would not be possible for me.
—I am terrified of anything that slithers. Sorry!
—Seriously, I cannot read a map. What if I get lost as we trek through? I would perish.
—They say I would have to build a shelter; I am not practical at all.

Further practice items
—What if you had an extra eye in the back of your head?
—Someone has suggested that all young people over the age of eight years must hold a paying job for five hours a week to get used to the idea of working. Do some black hat thinking on this. How many black hat points can you find, and what are they?
—People talk about each other a great deal. Sometimes, the things they say are true, sometimes untrue, and sometimes partly true (or exaggerated). People enjoy gossiping in this way, but what are the dangers and difficulties of this? Do some black hat thinking on this.

4.5  Yellow Hat Practice

Younger Learners

Going On a Journey!
The class is going on a trip to a local farm. Have the learners identify five key positives about what the trip could offer and how they might benefit from the experience.

Potential Responses
— It will be interesting to see the animals and learn more about them.
— The trip will help us learn about what it is like on a farm. I want to be a vet when I grow up, so I want to be able to learn more about what makes the animals sick.
— It will give me a chance to see animals up close for the first time. I might learn to be a bit braver if the farm workers help me feel safe.
— Being outside doing physical work will be a different experience.

My Report
It is the end of the year, and you ask the children to contribute to their own reports. What positives can they include about themselves that show the difference that their hard work has made? You might want to support them with key themes, such as learning, contributions to the class and their friends, confidence and concentration.

Potential Responses
— I am so much more positive now, especially in areas like maths and science. I go into each lesson to learn at least one new thing.
— I am doing less to achieve more. I used to get bogged down in the detail, and now, I try to keep things simple.
— My biggest achievement this year was breaking the school record for the 4 x 100 m relay. As a team, we listened to our teacher, worked hard and trained well.
— My project on conflict taught me how to understand and respect so many people I have never met.

Older Learners

Seeing Things Differently
A visitor who is blind is coming to the school to talk to the pupils about their experience as part of a whole-school project on seeing things from different perspectives. Before the visit, you ask the pupils to consider what some positives of being blind might be.

Potential Responses
— They may have sophisticated listening skills and may be resourceful when finding tools to help them, for example, audio tools and apps.
— They get to have a trained dog that they can take anywhere with them.
— In a world obsessed by image, they will value people using a range of criteria.
— Being able to use your other senses well to appreciate the world – listening to the birds and recognising their call or noticing the change in somebody's tone of voice when they are upset.

And Here's for Something Different

The drama/PE and art departments are collaborating to put on an entire-day workshop where local primary pupils can get involved in a range of activities.

What are five benefits the workshops must provide?

Potential Responses
— The pupils need to be able to have fun while straying out of their comfort zone, so the guidance must be clear.
— The pupils should use their skills and be included in the workshops.
— Pupils must have tried at least one new activity and felt a sense of success.
— The atmosphere must be joyful and positive, and all leaders need to always use positive communication.
— There should be an opening show performed by 'experts' to inspire awe and wonder and provide an opportunity for the younger pupils to perform for their school at the end of the day.

4.6 Green Hat Practice

Younger Learners

Celebrations
The bridge that crosses the river in your local village is said to be 500 years old. Locals decide to celebrate the bridge and ask the school to get involved in designing activities for the afternoon party. What suggestions could we make to the town council?

Potential Responses
— We could plan and advertise a walk for locals and visitors. It would start and end on the bridge. Local historians could tell us what they know. If we charge a small fee, that could help pay for some of the repairs that have to be made now and again.
— We could design and build model bridges for a display in the community centre. The winning design could be built on the school grounds.
— We could find a range of photographs of the bridge over time to see if it has changed. Using these, we could create a fact sheet, inviting local people to tell us their stories of the bridge. I know my granddad fished there when he was little.

What Happens Next with This Paint Palette?
Without leading the learners towards ideas of what might be painted, ask them to come up with as many ideas as they can within a specified time.

Potential Responses
— I think everybody in the room has to choose the same sort of colours that are on the palette and create something that they think is magical.
— The artist decided to go for a walk to get some inspiration.
— Are you going to ask us to paint exactly what we see? The palette?
— I am not sure, but do you want us to watch you paint and then guess what it might be?

Design an Invention
Invite learns to draw their designs for any of the following:
— A dog exercising machine
— A machine for weighing elephants
— A device for peeling vegetables

Older Learners

The Key, but to What?
They say that you have the key to unlocking your potential in your pocket. Using this metaphorical key, to think carefully about what you want your life to be like. What are the possibilities? Suppose every one of us is asked to leave school with part of our plan focused on 'giving something back'.

Potential Responses
— I see myself travelling the world, learning about other cultures and then using that knowledge in a profession that supports vulnerable people.
— My key would see me dancing, singing and performing acrobatics. I would make sure I thought of ways to visit schools, no matter how famous I became, for free and to inspire children just like I was inspired.
— I would be using technology to make life easier for older people. I would make sure that easily accessible and useful online resources were available.

Mystery Man

A man is walking down a busy street with a brown paper bag pulled over his head. Why is he doing this? What is going on? Write your ideas down. Try to give at least two possible explanations.

Potential Responses
— The man might be wearing the bag to win a bet.
— He might be trying to see what a blind person feels like.
— Maybe he doesn't like his new haircut.
— It might be a publicity stunt.
— He might be a walking advertisement for brown paper bags.
— He might be promoting the use of recyclable packaging.
— Maybe he is wearing the bag so that he won't be recognised. He might be famous or an escaped convict. Perhaps he owes someone money.

4.7 Blue Hat Practice

Younger Learners – Planning

Let's Talk
Ask the learners to use the Six Thinking Hats to write and perform a script, imagining they are interviewing a real-life hero whose story they will be presenting to their to parents. What questions might they ask?

Potential Response
- 🎩 What was special about your childhood?
- 🎩 How do you feel about the work you do?
- 🎩 What benefits does your work bring to others?
- 🎩 What are the risks of the work you do?
- 🎩 What are your dreams for the future, and what are the possibilities for your work?
- 🎩 What is your plan, and what actions could we take to help?

A Little Help for Our Friends
Every week, you encourage a challenge into the classroom that, if solved, could benefit a person or place.

Today's issue is one of loneliness. A learner's grandmother lives alone. She has many hobbies, such as reading, knitting, gardening and embroidery, and keeps herself busy in her house, cleaning and cooking. However, she experiences pain in her hands and might have to stop doing the hobbies she loves. They have been her passion for 75 years. What might help?

Set a time limit and have the learners use the blue hat to select three hats to use when thinking about this problem. Learners should stick to discussing the choice of hats used and **not the topic**. Then, have the learners compare ideas with another group, sharing their reasoning before presenting the ideas to the class for a final decision on the process.

Younger Learners – Summarising

Pole Position
Your grandparents have decided to help you build a racetrack in the garden from a range of materials found in the garage. The construction is not going completely to plan, and frustration is setting in. It is time to intervene.

— Let's use our blue hats to explore our thinking adventure so far.
— What is going well?
— What is not working?
— What needs to happen next?

The Writing Life
The school is establishing a pupils' monthly magazine relevant for the whole school. The editor has asked for learners who are interested in being part of the writing team to present a 'most interesting news report of the month' piece as part of the application process and prior to an interview. The editor has asked that

4. Additional Practice Topics

pupils choose a news item that they feel will interest and inform a wide range of people. They will need to summarise the contents and present it both in written form and verbally (during the interview) in a lively and engaging way.

NewsForKids.net – Real News, Told Simply.™

Younger Learners – Concluding

Out and About
Imagine you have been encouraging your learns to decide on the theme of the role-play area for the following term. Staff have presented three options that they believe will enhance the learning experience. The class has explored each of these ideas using the Six Thinking Hats method.

The teacher now asks all learners to put on their blue hats and prioritise each idea, focusing on potential engagement. Using her blue hat thinking, she states:

— I noted during the discussions that…
— Listening to your key points, I have identified that…
— So, finally, do we agree that …? Put on your blue hats and tell me what actions are required to make this happen.

https://www.teachingenglish.org.uk/article/role-play (Article)

With a Little Help from My Friend.
Learners have developed their approach to evaluating their own work towards self-improvement. Today, they have engaged in writing a sensory narrative linked to the previous day's visit from a nocturnal animal expert.

During the session, each learner should share their work with a peer who will wear their blue hat to summarise the overall impact of the writing. They will also conclude with a suggestion for further consideration. After both learners have had the opportunity to use their blue hat beneficially, they will consider the feedback, adapt and improve their narrative.

Goodbye, Mr C
The school's dearly loved headteacher is retiring. How will the learners celebrate the dedication he has demonstrated for 30 years? There is so much excitement and so many ideas that the discussion is becoming unstructured.

Ask for a pause in the proceedings, putting on your blue hat to explain the original purpose of the discussion and make explicit what is happening.

— Okay, let's take a few moments to summarise the content of the discussion so far.
— Have we balanced our thinking well enough?
— Let's record the strengths in our thinking to this point and identify how we might be restricting our plan?
— What do we do next?

Older Learners – Planning

Better to be Safe than Sorry
Learners spend a great deal of their time socialising online. The school is aware that the chances of learners experiencing cyberbullying are high and increase when learners lack the information to protect themselves.

A group of teachers are working with a range of community partners, including parents and the local police, to create a policy that communicates how learners of all ages can become more informed and reduce their online risk. They want learners to be a key part of the policy development, taking responsibility for ensuring it is relevant to their peers, pupil friendly, full of relevant information, appealing and useful.

Ask the learners which hats they might use to think about this and why?

Potential Responses
- ⬜ What information needs to be communicated?
- 🟢 Think of creative ways to communicate the information.
- 🔴 How do others feel about the topic and previous communication?
- 🟡 What is good about the way the information is communicated?
- ⚫ Are there any issues with how the information is communicated?
- 🔵 How will we know that we have been successful? What is the goal?

Older Learners – Summarising

My Business!
The school has introduced a mandatory syllabus that ensures all learners develop their entrepreneurial skills. Using clear success criteria each year group has identified their small business champions and the class generated idea to represent them in the 'board room'. We will take forward the project that fits the criteria most successfully and convincingly. The criterion for the business idea includes:

— Service to the community.
— Financial security.
— Ethical.
— Opportunity to develop the core skills of communication, thinking, interdependence, relevant use of technology and collaboration within and outside of the school environment, including the invitation to an expert.

In groups of six learners use a range of thinking to develop the first phase of their idea. A further group are neutral observers and serve as overall quality assurance for this initial phase of the project.

After all groups have presented their ideas, the teacher asks the observers to use their blue hat thinking to summarise their collective findings so far, against the given criterion.

— Does the project need further deliberation? If so, what are those further discussion points?

Getting the Facts Right – What Foods Are a Problem for Our Planet?
As an independent research activity and to support the school's approach towards global responsibility, learners will choose one website and contact one organisation then summarise their key points to support an overall summary for the school chef, who is adapting his menu considering up-to-date research on the impact of certain foods on the planet.

Older Learners – Concluding

Revisit
Revisit a topic you have previously covered but for which a conclusion was not reached. Ask the learners to summarise and conclude on the thinking.

A Restaurant

A restaurant decides to charge by time spent instead of for the food and service. You can eat as much as you like, but you are charged for the time you spend in the restaurant. Do some yellow hat thinking on this idea. List the benefits of the plan and reasons why it might work. Then do some black hat thinking to list the difficulties or problems – why it may not work. Finally, using the blue hat, conclude (a) whether you think the restaurant has a good idea and (b) what needs to happen next.

Sharing the Love

The school has decided that the annual fundraising event for this year will benefit three charities. You play a short video demonstrating the work of each charity and then ask the learners to collaborate with their parents to design and apply a thinking sequence to choose the charity that resonates with them the most.

Organisers will share the funds in proportion to the number of votes so that every vote counts and each charity benefits.

Here are some example charities you could include:
— The Oliver King Foundation | UK Charity For Defibrillator Access
— Devastating floods in Pakistan | UNICEF
— The British Hedgehog Preservation Society

As a guide for parents, you may want to scaffold the session by sending out the following questions as part of a planned structure, explaining the flexible approach if learners demonstrate a readiness for it:

- What are we aiming for at the end of our session?
- What do we know about the work of each charity and its capacity to survive. What motivates the charities? What else might we want to find out about?
- How do we feel about each charity? Let's gauge our motivation.
- What benefits would our donation provide?
- What are the possibilities regarding each charity's future work?
- How do we feel about each charity now?
- Summarise the discussion and agree on a decision and actions.

4.8
Additional Practice

Younger Learners

Our Edible Playground
A local gardener is working with a group of pupils to design an edible playground with hedges and flowers where birds and insects can thrive, which studies reveal is not happening now. The learners will introduce the thinking hats sequence to the gardener to begin the planning process and use his wisdom to the full. What sequence will work best as far as the gardener is concerned?

The Final Whistle
The school netball team is hosting the final match of the season and wins the regional cup. As hosts, the headteacher expects high behavioural standards from the school's team. Unfortunately, in response to the other team's impolite reaction to losing the match, a few of the girls on the host team respond inappropriately. The headteacher insists on a visit to the visiting school to apologise on behalf of the school. As you can imagine, there are a variety of initial reactions to this decision. Have the learners develop a thinking sequence for resolving the conflict.

Small Changes, Big Dreams
Discuss some small changes that have had an impact on your life in a big way. Feel free to use your own ideas or refigure others using your green hat thinking. Have fun!

Ask learners to share five of their own thoughts. Have them develop a thinking hat sequence to evaluate the impact of each change for its potential to change their lives for the better. How might they prioritise this impact?

— I went to a party that I didn't want to attend and where I met my best friend.
— Buying a pair of running shoes led me to running my first cross country and introduced me to a sport I love as well as all the health benefits it gives me.
— Taking the time to say hello and being kind to a newcomer in school led to an amazing friendship.
— Talking to the elderly lady who lives alone next door has introduced me to the wonders of gardening.
— Teaching my grandmother how to use the camera on her phone when I call means we make contact every day now and she can see me.

Saying Goodbye
Young people experience loss, either vicariously through the news or in their own lives. Plan a sequence that allows them to explore a way to value life when saying goodbye.

Older Learners

PIT Stop
You are introducing a different approach to homework, and the learners' parents are generally in favour of it. Personal interest topics and the development of a range of skills will be the focuses. The requirements for success will be as follows:

— Evidence-based research
— Consultation with an 'expert'
— A range of presentation styles
— Inclusion of a range of essential skills – collaboration, communication, reading, writing, mathematics, investigation and creativity

Have the learners plan and evaluate a PIT stop project using a predetermined thinking hats sequence.

Formula for Fun
Pose the following challenge to your learners:
Your parents want to host a Formula 1 Family Fun Day. The challenge will be to ensuring that motor enthusiasts as well as people who are not fans of the sport have an enjoyable afternoon and get involved. You have a budget of £200 to spend.
Develop a thinking hat sequence that you believe will offer the best possible chance for success and comes in at or under the budget.

Travelling Abroad
There is an opportunity for eight learners to take part in a school visit to Finland. They will experience a range of cultures, as learners from four other schools will also be attending the event. Invite the learners to design a thinking sequence to make the selection. This will be shared this with the governors, who are insisting that the process be well considered and fair.

Spooky Schools
There is a sleepover at the school to raise money for a local homeless charity while also celebrating Halloween. You want to plan the evening so that the learners enjoy themselves and are not afraid while also keeping the atmosphere 'alive'. Ask them to help you plan the structure of a thinking session so that all of their ideas and concerns about the event are addressed.

Food, Glorious Food
The school council are considering a suger free lunch menu. This includes removing all unhealthy dessert options. Ask learners to design a sequence of hats to explore this idea.

Bee Happy!
There is scientific evidence that bumblebees are not only diligent workers but also love to play. Show the learners a video (https://youtu.be/Nh4a137OU_Y) and supplement the information with just enough narrative to stimulate them.

Explain that they will be designing an experiment to evaluate this evidence. However, first, they need to plan their thinking. As individuals, they can spend a few minutes using their 'individual hat packs' to decide on the approach they might take.
Ask for feedback on the best experimental approach to take. Ensure you state that different scenarios are valid if they are reasoned effectively.
Ask the groups to collaborate on the activity now. Agreeing a hat sequence and assigning relevant questions to each hat.

- What are we thinking about? What do we need to think about next?
- What do we already know? What has been achieved before? What information do we still need?
- What could we do? Has anybody got any more ideas?

Given the same stimulus, ask the groups to use the material provided and devise a Six Thinking Hats sequence to develop an experiment aimed at proving that the bees' play activities did lead to evidence of contribution to survival strategies. Encourage individuals to think through this first before contributing their ideas to the whole group.

4.9
Additional Practice for Families

⬜ White Hat

Looking after the Pennies
As a family, the decision has been made to reduce the amount of spending on food and heating bills. The discussion has also included the need to be aware of waste and make different decisions to be more economical.

Questions to Support the Discussion.
— What facts about current spending do you already know?
— Are there any facts that support you in identifying where you waste energy, food and money?
— What information is missing?

Potential Response
— Our spending on food has gone up by 25% in the last year. That is the equivalent of…
— If we don't do something soon, we are not going to be able to afford the summer holiday that you all love.
— I leave my light on when I go to school, and it is still on when I get home. I wonder how much energy that wastes.

🟥 Red Hat

Work, Rest and Play
Your parents have decided that you are cramming too much into your schedule and are not living a healthy balanced life. They have asked you to identify one out-of-school activity that you could give up, making space for a time of rest.

Questions to Support the Discussion
— How do you feel about this decision?
— What words sum up what is going on for you right now?
— What colour best describes how this decision is landing with you?

Potential Response
— I am so mad I cannot talk to you right now.
— Great! More time for television.
— I am feeling controlled and like I really want to break free.

⬛ Black Hat

Camping in the Bathroom
A young family member wants to camp in the bathroom. You ask them to use the black hat constructively. What issues can they identify? How can they have fun with their camp and avoid preventing everyone else from using the bathroom?

Potential Response
—Someone else might want to use the bathroom when I am camping.
—My camp might get in the way.
—People might trip over things.
—Bathroom things might be difficult to find.

You could then use the green hat to address these issues.

Yellow Hat

Sun, Sea and Smiles
Your family and another family are planning a holiday together. You realise that there will be vastly different expectations, as the families are so different, but are asked to see the potential benefits.

Questions to Support the Discussion
—Give me at least one potential positive outcome of the holiday.
—What are the qualities we have as a family that could help make this situation work?
—What positive contribution would each of us like to make to ensure at least one person has a better-than-expected time?

Potential Response
—Gosh, I never knew we were so cool.
—Okay, this could work.
—This will make me a better person.

Green Hat

Team Tactics
Times are changing. As the younger members of the family are now in school and both parents are now working, there is a need to share some of the daily responsibilities. It is time to get creative and think of a range of creative opportunities to solve this issue.

Questions to Support the Discussion
—How could we divide the responsibilities so that everyone is happy?
—What could be a great next step?
—Who has some wacky ideas? Could we look at things differently?

Potential Response
—Could we work it so that we had a weekend off every couple of weeks?
—We could all pick a chore out of the hat each morning.
—We could do the same chore each day so that we get great at it and really fast.

Blue Hat

Paint Me a Picture
Your sister is having difficulty with her art teacher, and it is having an impact on her work, happiness and health. Time for a family discussion to help prepare her for a conversation with the teacher planned for the following week.

Questions to Support the Conversation Planning

🟦 Using our blue hat, what is the best possible outcome of the meeting? What do we need to consider next? Let's put a sequence together.

Potential Responses

- ⬛ What are the challenges now?
- 🟥 How do those make you feel?
- 🟨 What are the benefits of working with this teacher?
- 🟩 How might we change things to increase those benefits?
- 🟦 Let's summarise what we have said so far.
- 🟥 How do you feel now?
- 🟦 What have we learned?

Milton Keynes UK
Ingram Content Group UK Ltd.
UKHW051943050424
440655UK00005B/32

9 781739 789329